THE ANATOMY OF POWER

Also by James Margach

HOW PARLIAMENT WORKS
SIXTY YEARS OF POWER (WITH LORD SWINTON)
THE ABUSE OF POWER

The Anatomy of Power

*An Enquiry into
the Personality of Leadership*

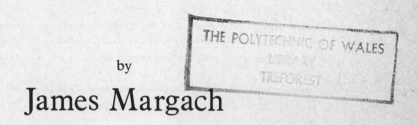

by

James Margach

W. H. ALLEN · LONDON
A Howard & Wyndham Company
1979

PUBLISHER'S NOTE

James Margach died on 23 March 1979, soon after handing in to us the book in its present form. We were to set the book and then James would make further corrections and additions, and obviously update the book in the light of the then forthcoming referenda in Wales and Scotland. Naturally he would have made changes following the General Election and the European Elections. However, the book has been left as he wrote it.

James Margach was also going to add a chapter to be called 'The Might-Have-Beens', but, alas, his notes were not far enough advanced for us to include anything in this volume. We would have loved to have read James's reactions and comments on those who almost became Prime Minister!

We know that James was very pleased with the long chapter called 'The Lobby' and think it is a fitting memorial to him.

Printed and bound in Great Britain by
REDWOOD BURN LIMITED
Trowbridge & Esher

for the Publisher, W. H. Allen & Co. Ltd.,
44 Hill Street, London W1X 8LB.

ISBN 0 491 02269 7

Contents

Introduction

TWELVE
PRIME MINISTERS

Winston Churchill once said that 'we are a nation of short memories'. Already we have forgotten that only the day before yesterday we were the mightiest Empire the world has ever known. My purpose in writing this book as a newspaperman, after 45 years in Westminster's salt-mines, is to tell what it was all like when we were at the top of the world league before we were relegated and found ourselves halfway down the second division. And to tell of the twelve Prime Ministers, when I knew them as they really were in flesh and blood, at the peak of their powers,* not as the cardboard figures they emerge as at the hands of people who never knew them. An old hand finds it difficult to recognise them as they are reconstructed. The real personalities differed greatly from the public persona dressed up in diaries and shaped by biographies. The danger comes when the central characters start believing the myths and legends, packaged like corn-flakes or cans of beer by their public relations salesmen. From my advantageous front-row seat I saw them in action at the time, when the heat was on. That is when one sees big men become smaller and others, who started out under-rated as small men, visibly grow in stature.

Politics is about power. Power is about people. People are personalities. So I have tried to group the dozen Premiers as they appeared to me at the time, as they played their party roles in the grand theatre of politics, in relation to each other in the Anatomy of Power and the Personality of Leadership: not seen or judged in isolation but in the continuing narrative of history. By this means it has been possible to discard the boredom of policies and the side-shows of party politics and to see our great men in terms of the essential qualities which go to make up the elusive power of leadership. These qualities one rates as luck, ambition, courage, vision and

---

* With the exception of David Lloyd George (later Earl Lloyd-George). Lloyd George left office in 1922, never to return, but he remained a powerful force on the Parliamentary scene almost until his death in 1945.

idealism, management, and ruthlessness and cruelty when even Prime Ministers are never squeamish in using the razor to disfigure or wipe out others and at the same time save their own skins. After a half-century on the circuit I am convinced that the great indefinables in power have little to do with economics, currencies, massive legislative Bills, or manifesto pledges, but with the inner personality impulses like emotions, nerves, visions and dreams—the elusive psyche factors. In short, Prime Ministers as human beings.

Most of them by now have already become encrusted by the frequent artificial interpretation and distortions of instant history. Indeed, they have all suffered from this mistaken image, not least Winston Churchill himself. For this reason I have devoted a major chapter to dispose of the totally false picture presented for history of Churchill in the inter-war years. As part of the urge for escapism he is seen as the folk-hero leader of an all-party mass movement clamouring for tough action to halt Hitler and Mussolini; and that he was only frustrated as the voice of popular will by the 'guilty men' like Neville Chamberlain and others. This is a grotesque distortion of what really happened. A veteran newsman's clear memory and his notebooks and cuttings of the period confirm that Churchill was the loneliest and most despised and rejected of men, the most unpopular man conceivable. He had only four truly loyal friends,* for nobody wanted to know him or be associated with him. Indeed, plans were far advanced in his Epping constituency to ditch him, to kick him out of Parliament and party, and replace him by an appeasing party loyalist. The wilderness awaited him in loneliness. The great irony of history is that Winston Churchill was preserved for Britain and human freedom by Hitler's invasion of Poland in September 1939. It was German aggression that effectively halted the campaign, then rolling strongly, to throw him to the wolves in Epping. It is odd how a people's guilt conscience can give an artificial slant to history.

Because I am the only Palace of Westminster journalist survivor from the inter-war years, I am persuaded to try to recapture the scene when we were a great Empire and Westminster was the political centre of the world before its rapid decline set in. Generations have grown to maturity to whom the British story in the global adventure of power is almost unknown and certainly little understood. They are curious to know what it all looked like. So I have tried to tell the story of an eye-witness of what Imperial grandeur and majesty was like at Westminster, what Parliament really was then, the type of parties and elites that ruled on the Labour as well as on the Conservative benches; what Parliament was really like in close-up and what happened daily then (compared with now) when

* See Chapter 8, p. 112.

Britain was at her apogee of dominion over five continents and seven oceans—before loss of Empire and the rape by the Executive, that crossbreed of Government and bureaucracy, removed all power from Westminster. The Westminster Parliament was then the greatest democratic assembly in the world. It is in grave danger of ending up as a power vacuum with more power in transit to the new Assemblies and Parliaments in Edinburgh, Cardiff, Strasbourg, Luxembourg and Brussels.

Finally, I make no apology for devoting a substantial chapter to the mystique, working customs and future of 'The Lobby'—Westminster's media men and women who are the privileged (though not in the parliamentary sense) outsiders operating as insiders in constant contact with Government, Whitehall, and politics. Here my story is not only concerned with the astonishing growth of Whitehall's massive Information Service, from the 'one man and his dog' when I started out to the present army of 1,500-plus, fortified by a mass technical and servicing network. The issues are much more important and formidable, for these are central to the exercise of power and the healthy working of the democratic system. Government by information and publicity is already the key weapon in the armoury at the exclusive disposal of the Executive. Inevitably this will become more massive and powerful, for within itself it has the momentum and mechanism to grow faster. This is the key to future growth and power, inevitably involving more and more manipulation of information and opinion and the sophisticated techniques of news-management, reinforced by the freedom of decision on timing, release, and how much should be disclosed. The role of Information in the modern highly complex world of communications is clearly going to be still more powerful, notably in the area of secrecy. Yet the sophisticated exercise of communications controlled by the State is the least researched and debated sector of power. So one who was in at the start of this transformation in power structure needs no excuses for opening it up. I am warned that this is the first time that the Lobby story has been told from the inside. I have no guilt complex, because I know I have the goodwill of all the new and younger generations of political correspondents at Westminster in pulling aside some of the veils and debating the problems and dangers ahead.

The journey has been exciting and moving, tragic and exhilarating. I do not draw on theory and learning, only on experience and life, as it happened at the time. My own presence provides the continuity and connecting link. I offer no excuses, only one explanation. At least I was there.

James Margach.

I

THE PERSONALITY OF LEADERSHIP

Many personal qualities and forces are indispensable for great leadership. Ambition is the most compulsive and integral, for without this spur the newly discovered leader would never even be around when events and opportunities herald the rendezvous. Without ambition the pursuit of fame would never prevail. 'I love fame,' Disraeli said. 'Ambition is the motive power,' said Churchill. Courage, too, is among the highest qualities, for without moral courage and native guts the hammer blows of disaster could not be suffered or survived. Churchill claimed that courage is the 'quality that guarantees all others.' My case-book confirms that when courage cracks under strain the leader ends up a nervous wreck—and it would have been better if he had never received the Sovereign's commission. With courage must go character. The sophisticated packaging by advertising and public relations experts may succeed temporarily in creating illusion by cardboard images, but first Parliament and then the public have an instinct for detecting defects and counterfeits in character. Stamina is essential, because the glittering prizes of history seldom go to the sprinter but to the stayer. A leader will never make the list for final selection without patience. With patience goes the capacity for judgment, not only of policies but of men, in assessing the tare weight or Plimsoll Line which colleagues can safely stand without sinking. Finally, one must pay great respect to the opinion of experts, top Ministers who have served in many Cabinets under different Prime Ministers, and Permanent Secretaries who have dealt with the great men whose public masks have been left in the outer office. They place ruthlessness at or near the top of the league. In their judgment, great leaders must be ruthless in reaching decisions and dealing with colleagues, however dear or close, *after* they have grabbed control of all the levers of power. This is the indispensable hardening ingredient for character. A great leader must never be squeamish at the sight of blood, other people's blood, when he reaches the top of Disraeli's greasy pole.

But ambition, courage, ruthelessness, the pursuit of fame, character, vision, judgment, patience, stamina are all essential qualities which constitute the Personality of Leadership *after* the Prime Minister gets into No 10 Downing Street. For my money the most precious asset *before* he makes it is luck, and here I draw only on life and experience at first-hand, not on academic theory at second. So I can confirm that all but two of the dozen Prime Ministers, and a couple of Opposition leaders, whom I knew well, would never have reached the top without having been blessed with incredibly good fortune for themselves, coinciding with the misfortunes of their rivals and sometimes of the country as well. That provides the clue to the Anatomy of Leadership and the essential key to the exercise of power. The secret of power lies in how the great men exploit their luck once they get there, by displaying qualities of greatness and growth which nobody ever suspected and, in a few cases, exhibiting weaknesses which cheer leaders in Parliament, parties and media had overlooked in their over-sell. Like Napoleon's marshals, to be lucky is the precondition to getting there, alike as to Prime Minister and party leader. The accident-prone never make it.

LUCK OF THE DRAW

Let our two contemporaries head the list of the lucky ones. Neither James Callaghan nor Margaret Thatcher would have reached their current eminence if they had not shared exceptionally good fortune in being dealt the strongest trump cards when the power-bids were called. Callaghan indeed rated his chances of ever becoming Prime Minister and party leader as so remote and unrealistic that he was ready and anxious to contract out of British public life altogether in May 1973. Then it was he decided to leave Westminster for good, say farewell to all future prospects of glory and a plinth in history, and accept the job as Secretary-General of the International Monetary Fund based in Washington. His appointment was all lined up, with powerful international backing, but with the approval of only France outstanding. But President Pompidou and Giscard d'Estaing, France's Finance Secretary, vetoed him. They informed other Presidents and Prime Ministers that Callaghan was unacceptable, not because they feared that Labour's former Chancellor might prove to be an inefficient secretary but because they did not like the prospect of the Anglo-Americans running the IMF. So Callaghan had to soldier on at Westminster. His stock was then so low that nobody would have included him even as a long shot among the half-dozen front-runners to succeed Harold Wilson. He held on, kept his head down, and instead of being the

2

forgotten man of yesterday behind a Washington desk he had a runaway victory three years later when he became Prime Minister. He was also lucky that Wilson decided to retire at the precise moment when Callaghan was at his most powerful inside the Labour Government and Party. He was fortunate also that he satisfied the mood of the Labour Party and trade unions at that particular moment; after the tantrums, controversies and bad odour of the Wilson era they rallied massively behind Callaghan as the best man to restore character, bottom and solid qualities and standards.

TIMING

Margaret Thatcher displayed high qualities of personal courage when *she* decided to stand against Edward Heath for the leadership of the Conservative Party. She could not have been luckier both in timing and in her rivals. If Heath had resigned immediately on being defeated after the second 1974 election, when it was clear the mood of the party wanted rid of him, William Whitelaw would have been accepted as the new leader with solid support. But Heath hung on, and when it was clear he was determined to fight back against the campaign to overthrow him Whitelaw decided not to run against his leader in the first round, because of old-style chivalry; he felt it would not be honourable conduct in the mess if the second-in-command were to seek to get his commanding officer reduced in rank. But in the second round? . . . By then honour and loyalty would be satisfied, and he would be prepared to be drafted. But the bell never rang for him in the second round, which proved a formality. Mrs Thatcher won impressively by a knock out because of her formidable lead in the first. This was splendid luck for her. She proved ruthless in her conviction that Heath had to be replaced. Whitelaw, by comparison, lacked her courage and ruthlessness. He forgot one of the basic lessons of power. There is no friendship at the very top. The killer's instinct alone ensures survival in the jungle. Margaret Thatcher proved a killer. She won.

James Callaghan was not the first Prime Minister to reach No 10 Downing Street after an earlier decision to quit politics, convinced that he had no future in high office. Sir Henry Campbell-Bannerman, who formed the great Liberal Government in 1905—acknowledged by historians to be the greatest Government with all the talents of brilliance and genius in this century—modestly wrote himself off in 1895 as unlikely ever to get even mid-tier office and made strenuous efforts to become Mr Speaker. He failed to get enough support for the Commons chair. But ten years later he was acclaimed as an impressive Prime Minister, in his flair for running such a highly geared team. As Clement Attlee saw his own role forty years after Campbell-Bannerman, in the cricket jargon he

3

liked: 'You don't need to be a master-batsman forever scoring centuries or a demon bowler skittling out the other side to be a great captain in the field when the pressure is at its height.'

THE MAN IN POSSESSION

Attlee, whose stature and achievements as a Prime Minister have increased enormously with the passage of time, was exceptionally lucky, one of the luckiest among the many lucky leaders in our gallery. He not only captured the leadership when nobody was looking, but having been given the leading role as a stand-in when an entire Cabinet was wiped out in the early thirties, he proceeded to show cold ruthlessness by holding on to what he had got by accident when all the stars with more famous names returned to the cast. His was an extraordinary show of bloody-mindedness in one most people saw as a timid little mouse. First, he had the great good luck to be one of the fifty Labour MPs who survived the 1931 massacre. George Lansbury became leader of a platoon because, as the former Commissioner of Works, he was the most senior surviving Minister left from the defeated Labour Government; and Attlee became deputy-leader because he had been Postmaster-General. When Lansbury was compelled to resign by the trade unions—in Ernest Bevin's phrase, for 'hawking his pacifist conscience from meeting to meeting, asking people what he should do with it'—Attlee succeeded as leader. Despite the fact that most of the big names from the former Labour Cabinet had returned at the 1935 general election, Attlee held on and was elected leader as the man in possession, beating off all his rivals with prior claims, like Herbert Morrison, Arthur Greenwood, J. R. Clynes. It was an astonishing stroke of luck for Attlee. I remember clearly how dumbfounded we all were on the night. Labour had opted for the most colourless and unimpressive figure available. After Ramsay MacDonald, with his magnetic personality and rolling purple passages in the Gladstone tradition, they elected a leader without personality who could speak only in short staccato sentences without even verbs.

After him, the next Labour Prime Minister, Harold Wilson, owed everything to luck—and the tragedies of others. But for the premature deaths of Hugh Gaitskell and Aneurin Bevan, leader and deputy leader, he would have earned only footnotes in history. The vacancy for the leadership on Gaitskell's death, making Wilson's accession to the Premiership possible, could not have come at a more fortuitous moment, just when a great many Labour MPs were starting to take a closer look at the excitable tantrums and scene-creating histrionics of George Brown, the deputy leader and the heir-apparent to Gaitskell's tradition. 'Better George Brown drunk than Harold Wilson sober,' was *The Times* tart heading to

4

a critical leading article many years later, during a Labour Government crisis.

Wilson possessed a quicksilver instinct for knowing how to exploit his great stroke of luck. I was interviewing him for my paper, *The Sunday Times*, on the Friday afternoon when the final results were coming in for the cliff-hanger 1964 general election. With only a few results outstanding, a Labour victory in a Yorkshire constituency was flashed on the screen. It guaranteed him a majority of one (later results increased it to four). At once he started changing into formal dress and striped pants ready to go to the Palace to receive the Queen's commission to form a Labour Government. 'But you've a majority of only one,' I pointed out, 'you can't keep a Government going by the skin of your nose.' His response proved he was a gambler as well. 'I'll pilot it by the seat of my pants then,' he replied. 'The main thing is to get in there, form a Government and then control events and time the next election.' He capitalised his luck with undoubted courage and an incredible flair and ingenuity in a dangerous situation; he made politics exciting. This was Wilson's best period, before he lost his way by too much gimmickry and 'instant Government' off the cuff.

Good luck also chose the first of Labour's four Prime Ministers, Ramsay MacDonald, whose role as the creator, organiser and inspirer of the party has never been adequately recognised because he has been the handy peg on which to hang so many escapist myths. He shared the good fortune of his three successors, in the sense that he won the leadership unexpectedly against all the odds, form and the pundits' prophecies. On 21 November, 1922, at the first party meeting after the general election, he was elected party leader by a majority of only five votes over J. R. Clynes, who had been party leader and chairman for four years. The surprise was all the greater because MacDonald had not even been an MP for four years: he lost his Leicester seat because of the backlash for his critical stance during the First World War. His lucky election by such a narrow squeak over a 'father figure' was due to the impact at Westminster for the first time of a score of 'Red Clydesiders' who voted solidly for Ramsay because he was one of their ilk in the Independent Labour Party. There was a hang-over of this behaviour-pattern among the militants forty years later when Harold Wilson defeated the form favourite, George Brown, because of the solid Left-Wing Bevanite vote, whereas the post-Gaitskellite Right-Centre groupings split.

DESTRUCTION OF LLOYD GEORGE
Three of the Conservative Prime Ministers in my gallery also reached the summit of power only as the result of phenomenal luck in a totally unex-

5

pected combinations of circumstances. Stanley Baldwin, who was the effective Prime Minister for fifteen years, alike in substance and as shadow, owed this staggering ascendancy to a brief, pungent, unprepared, speech of a few minutes only which he delivered at the famous Carlton Club meeting which destroyed Lloyd George and sentenced him to the political wilderness for the remaining twenty-three years of his life and ended the war-time Coalition Government, leading to a Conservative Government immediately. At the same time, the Carlton Club rebellion produced another stroke of good fortune for Baldwin. It isolated all the glamorous and senior Conservatives and dynamic personalities who remained loyal to Lloyd George. By this lucky chance—he was an almost unknown figure—his succession as Prime Minister and party leader became possible when Bonar Law died of cancer before a year was out. Baldwin confessed years later: 'The position of leader came to me when I was inexperienced, by a succession of curious chances which could not have been foreseen. We have just buried the Unknown Prime Minister beside the Unknown Soldier,' he said, leaving the funeral service for Bonar Law at Westminster Abbey. Baldwin himself was the most unexpected Prime Minister of all time. His principal rival, Lord Curzon, wrote when Baldwin became leader and Prime Minister: 'A man of no experience and of the utmost insignificance—not even a public figure.' The moral stands the test of the years: beware of misguided snap judgments of surprise leaders who arrive from nowhere. That was how the most successful and best all-round peace-time Prime Minister of the twentieth century, in the judgment of this political newsman, was discovered. He had the supreme political skills and native cunning to exploit all the lucky breaks that came his way. History loves to honour born winners. Losers are forgotten with the morning papers. 'I would rather take a single ticket to Siberia than become Prime Minister,' Baldwin had said. Ambition and vision combined to keep him away from the booking hall at Victoria station.

History wrote the same scenario for Harold Macmillan, whom I rate as closest to Baldwin among the Prime Ministers I knew. He was so very much like Baldwin. They were superb political masters; they shared the identical qualities which enabled them to tower over their rivals and contemporaries, not least in their Celtic imagery, imagination and insight, always reserving the grand entry and performance for the big occasion. My Lowland Scot's tribute to the Highland strain derives from close study over many years. 'The English will never understand him,' said Lloyd George of Baldwin, 'he's one of us' meaning the Celts. Ramsay MacDonald shared the same Celtic qualities of the other three. This perhaps explains their staying power. Others, like Chamberlain,

6

Eden, cracked early on. Macmillan was one of the luckiest among the many lucky PMs. He was for sixteen years a backbencher, without even minor office; and it was only when Churchill formed his war-time Coalition that he was given his first ministerial job. When he was Chancellor of the Exchequer it seemed he was advancing towards honourable retirement, because his Prime Minister, Eden, was over three years younger. So by normal tests Macmillan had reached his ceiling had Eden had an average run. Macmillan's situation was captured by Harold Wilson, then Shadow Chancellor: 'Collect your Viscountcy and go' (though at the end of the journey Macmillan proved less susceptible to garters and ermine than Wilson). When Eden crashed in health and resigned over Suez, Macmillan was preferred to R. A. Butler because the Tories believed he had shown tougher mettle in Britain's last fling at Imperial glory. This was not so. It was not generally known that it was Macmillan who had put the skids under Eden: he threatened to resign if Eden refused to crush President Nasser by force, and then, as Chancellor, gave Eden the ultimatum that unless the Suez invasion was called off in twenty-four hours the pound would be wrecked and the economy ruined. Macmillan is the best example of how an ambitious man should play his hand aggresively once fate has dealt him the lucky cards. There lies the secret in the exercise of power, knowing what to do with it when unexpectedly you are presented with it. Macmillan was an artist in its use.

Macmillan's successor, on the other extreme, had not a clue what to do with power when it was pushed upon him unsought. He was the last amateur gentleman, measured by the old tests, ever likely to be at No 10, the aristocrat produced by fourteen generations of elitist breeding. Considering how many hearts have been broken in the pursuit of the glittering prize, Douglas-Home was unique: he never lifted a finger to grab the Premiership, it was presented to him on a plate; he had never had occasion to think how the Prime Minister does the job, he never sought to hold on to it once he realised that many in the party wanted him to go and make way for abrasive pace-setter Edward Heath. There has been nothing quite like the brief Douglas-Home episode on record. The party rejected two men desperately yearning for the crown, Lord Hailsham, who threw away his excellent chance of succeeding Macmillan by 'blowing his top', ostentatiously flinging his hat in the ring, and putting on a circus show; and there was 'Rab' Butler, reluctant to appear over-keen, again denied the crown, despite the fact that he had done more to reshape, modernise and liberalise the Conservative Party for the second half of the twentieth century than the five Prime Ministers whom he had served with such distinction and devotion. Douglas-Home was the only Prime Minister I knew who was a happy man to surrender the job; he was

7

free of that ambition which destroys so many more brilliant men; he had commonsense, that most uncommon of qualities, and he was happier with his trout-flies, the rod, gun, roses and his dogs than with the political squabbling of the market place. He got the leadership by luck and accident. As the fourteenth earl he knew what was the conduct required when informed that the party wanted a change. His successor was treated altogether differently.

CHANGING FACE OF TORYISM

Once Douglas-Home realised that the young Turks wanted him to go he dwelt not upon the manner of his going but went. Ted Heath was lucky. The Tories were in the mood to swing from the high breeding of the great aristocratic families with rolling acres and grouse moors to the lower middle-class artisan breeding with a mere third-acre at the back of the semi-detached. Heath fitted the bill as to the manner born by breeding. Basically, the party wanted a Tory Wilson, a grammar school-boy who, like Labour's leader, had been to Oxford too for finishing. Heath was the identikit model for the abrasive pace-setters who were supposed to be on the voters' rolls in their millions. Heath's experience provides an insight into the temper and memory of politics. When the campaign was being mounted to run Douglas-Home out of town the only man who could have called off the pack was Heath, the rebels' favourite son. He did not do so. In due course, after his record as a three-time election loser, the party got in the mood for yet another change. This time he was at the receiving end; so many of the new generation were clambering on the Thatcher bandwagon that few of his old friends were left to save his honour and pride. That's politics in the raw. The media create the illusion that Labour is always in a leadership crisis, but the party seldom overthrows its leaders; the Conservatives, by comparison, are ruthless and merciless in sacrificing leaders. Few have been lucky enough to go happily, freely, in their own time.

There are two notable exceptions to this story of how luck plays the principal role in plucking potential Premiers and party leaders from the shadows, often in the most surprising combination of circumstances as we have seen. But there was nothing lucky or haphazard about the succession of Neville Chamberlain and Anthony Eden. Each had been the Crown Prince for many years, each had shown at times great impatience under the strain of waiting for the call. No electoral colleges or magic circles were necessary for their ascent to the top of the greasy poll, which was accomplished as by right, without challenge or rivals, but with universal acclaim. Yet they both proved tragic failures. Neither enjoyed lucky breaks. Appeasement destroyed Chamberlain, Suez destroyed

Eden. Both were cruelly despised and rejected, without sympathy or tears, the most sickening instances of political regicide in living memory. Yet they both became Prime Ministers with more popular enthusiasm than was spared for the rest of the Premiers this century. Exceptionally, too, they were the creatures of their party, created in its image. In return, they were both obsessed by party loyalty. By comparison, Churchill, Baldwin and Macmillan were guilty of piracy and high treason—but they proved the lucky ones. That is how great leadership is created, notably when it is much more widely based than party.

Even the colossi, Lloyd George and Winston Churchill, despite the inevitability of their destiny as warrior-statesmen and saviours of their country, owed much to luck. Lloyd George was fortunate that the Prime Minister he overthrew and succeeded, as the result of considerable intrigue, Asquith, had been Prime Minister continuously for seven years, was tired and in no shape to fight his challenger. An exhausted man— Asquith was referred to as 'Squiff' in the diaries and letters of the period because of his dependence upon liquor to sustain him—was that much easier to supersede in consequence. Winston Churchill would never have held office again in the Conservative Party, let alone become party leader and Premier, but for the Second World War. Throughout the inter-war years,* he was written off as a dangerous and erratic genius, a man with a past but no future. Even in one of the earliest crises of the war, on the overthrow of Neville Chamberlain, the mass of Conservatives still did not want him as Prime Minister and party leader; it was only Attlee's insistence that it had to be Winston and not Lord Halifax (Attlee's first choice), as a condition for Labour's joining a Coalition, that clinched it for him.

It can thus be seen that luck must be the pre-eminent factor for all Prime Ministers to enable them to reach No. 10 Downing Street in the first place. My own experience confirms that the inevitable never happens, the improbable and the unexpected always, the impossible repeats itself most of the time. These basic laws and guidelines of politics remain constant, no matter how often the stars and the props in the theatre of politics may be changed. And after the improbable and the impossible? Only then can the potential qualities of leadership, and even statesmanship in a very few cases, be measured as the inter-action of and reaction of power on personalities. As Churchill said to Lloyd George—and one cannot seek higher authority: 'Most men sink into insignificance when they quit office, insignificant men acquire weight when they obtain it.' At the time they were discussing Bonar Law, the Conservative leader and Prime Minister, who had mastered them both. The lessons of history

* See Chapter 8, Churchill: The Myth and the Facts.

are overwhelming. However lucky a man may be in becoming Prime Minister and party leader, if he possesses the qualities of leadership underneath, his personality will bloom with the job. Defoe claimed that any Prime Minister must of necessity be an egotist and an autocrat, and added: 'If he comes to office without these characteristics his environment equips him with them as surely as a diet of royal jelly transforms a worker into a queen bee.'

Now to see how the diet works when prescribed.

PARAMOUNTCY OF COURAGE

It is only after Lady Luck has dealt the cards that the real tests and the true values of the Personality of Leadership in politics can be measured. For it is in the *exercise* of power after it has been acquired that the qualities of courage, ambition, patience, vision, ruthlessness and stamina of the Prime Ministers can be discovered and tested. Perhaps the principal lesson to be drawn from one's first-hand experience of the twelve Prime Ministers reviewed in this book is that the outstanding successes among them were the unexpected outsiders, often unknowns, who brushed aside more fashionable rivals. They confounded the pundits' prophecies about the certainties of form, and mocked the judgments of instant history. On the other hand, the most calamitous failures, responsible for catastrophes of the first magnitude, were the Crown Princes who became party leaders and Premiers by natural succession and right of inheritance. This paradox in the Anatomy of Power was described by Asquith, himself the last of the Romans, in his memorial address to honour his predecessor, Campbell-Bannerman. There have been men, said Asquith, 'who, in the cruel phrase of the ancient historian, were universally judged to be fit for the highest place only until they attained and held it. Our late Prime Minister belonged to that rarer class whose fitness for such a place, until they attain and hold it, is never adequately understood.'

In this second category there were three outstanding peace-time Prime Ministers in my time. Stanley Baldwin, Clement Attlee and Harold Macmillan reached the highest office in the most unexpected circumstances, thanks to lucky breaks. But once there they displayed an instant instinct for power and leadership. They possessed all the nobler qualities listed as prerequisites for success, but were also professionally adept in the baser techniques of cunning, calculation, intrigue and ruthlessness. They survived at the top with astonishing tenacity for incredibly long periods, the most remarkable considering that they were regarded as temporary incumbents, to be allowed only brief runs before inevitable defeat. 'Basking in obscurity,' wrote A. J. P. Taylor, in his *English History*, describing Baldwin's unexpected emergence at the top in 1922. 'A miserable depressing day,' wrote Hugh (later Lord) Dalton in his diary the night when Attlee was elected leader of the Labour Party; 'and a little mouse shall lead them.'*

Macmillan, as Chancellor in Anthony Eden's Government, appeared to have reached his ceiling and could reasonably start preparing to go out to grass. Eden's early smash-up brought him a new world of power he could never remotely have imagined; and even when he became Prime Minister we all regarded him as a temporary stand-in, the ideal man to lead the party into Opposition, after what seemed inevitable defeat. Baldwin and Attlee remained at the top for fifteen years, though not all the time as Premiers; Macmillan was Prime Minister continuously for seven years. Again history's partiality for winners; losers are mercilessly stripped of even the credit for their earlier achievements.

Courage was the pre-eminent quality these Prime Ministers possessed most powerfully. There were other qualities in their balanced personality in leadership, Celtic vision and imagery, beauty of eloquence, native cunning, and great skills in the endless adventure of managing men in the case of Baldwin and Macmillan; and patience, stamina, character and a streak of cruelty and cynicism in Attlee. The three of them were ruthless as butchers. But, above all else, their courage was herculean. The greatest of all, Lloyd George and Winston Churchill, possessed courage in historic grandeur and are beyond the tests applied to lesser mortals. But even the anatomy of courage reflected different shadings for them, too. Churchill cherished courage above all else, physical and moral. He rejoiced when exposing himself to danger where bombs were falling. Lloyd George had moral and political courage, reinforced with audacity and the passion of bravery in taking political risks, but of physical courage he had none. In both the First and Second World Wars he was terrified in air raids by the sound of gunfire. But his moral and political courage to inspire a battered nation was supreme. Another aspect of Lloyd George's political dynamism: he always went for the big game, preferably the lion, and never wasted time on smaller species.

BALDWIN'S PRE-EMINENCE

Of the three great Prime Ministers named above I am confident that Baldwin will be seen in history as pre-eminent in this century. The Baldwin Age identifies the impact of the Personality of Leadership in his case. Historians never write about the Age of Attlee or Macmillan or Wilson. None of the other Premiers come close to him in the astonishing hold he had on the affections of the country, something quite above party politics. Character and standards told decisively in his case, but his secret

* *The Fateful Years*, Hugh Dalton (Muller).

lay in the courage he showed in getting all the major decisions of his age right: India, the General Strike, the Abdication, routing the Press Lords Rothermere and Beaverbrook, overthrowing Lloyd George, modernising the Tory Party despite splits. He never exerted himself over secondary issues. The best tests of a Premier's courage often comes round the Cabinet table, and there he was the first of the independent Presidential-style Prime Ministers. This test came early on. In 1925 the Conservatives were clamouring for legislation to ban the levies paid by trade unions to the Labour Party and a Private Member's Bill was introduced to achieve this purpose, with overwhelming support. Baldwin summoned a special Cabinet to consider the Government's attitude, and asked each Minister to express his opinion.

All Ministers argued that the Bill must be supported and become law. Then Baldwin summed up and spelt out to his colleagues what he proposed to say in the debate. He would tell Parliament and the nation, he explained, that the Government was not prepared to use its massive majority to steamroller through a Bill which would provoke acute controversy and bitterness. He would ask his supporters, then in a militant mood for union-bashing, to make sacrifices for the good of the country. His view did not remotely represent his Cabinet's views. Ministers were astonished. Lord Birkenhead passed a note across the table. 'I think your action shows enormous courage and for that reason will succeed.' Austen Chamberlain wrote: 'He astonished me . . . I have bet Sam Hoare £5 that he will bring it off triumphantly.'*

Baldwin did bring if off triumphantly. Courage in being the odd man out in his Cabinet and then in defying the overwhelming opinion of his own party was the clue to his other qualities in leadership: character, vision, style, patience, judgment and timing.

The way in which a Prime Minister runs his Cabinet and leads his party *before* it is ready to follow is the clue to his inner confidence and courage. Compare Baldwin's style with Harold Wilson's. Richard Crossman in his diaries described a situation where the Labour Cabinet was evenly divided on a major issue. 'Harold said, "What shall I do, it's a tie?" I said *sotto voce*, "Be a Prime Minister" and Richard Marsh giggled. But Harold repeated plaintively, "What shall I do, it's a tie." He is a very strange man.'† On another occasion he feared he was to be overthrown by a coup by the moderates in his Cabinet over the controversial supply of arms to South Africa. He encouraged a round-robin motion by Labour MPs to support him; and if left too isolated in the Cabinet conceived the masterplan to resign as party leader and then stand for re-election. This

* *Baldwin*, Middlemas & Barnes (Weidenfeld).

† *Crossman Diaries* (Hamilton & Cape).

exposes the many refinements in leadership. Here Wilson was showing his superb mastery of the techniques in manipulation, but he was not showing courage, rather the raw ends of his over-taut nerves. Despite this example, one's instinct is that Wilson will be given a squarer deal by the next century's historians than the harsh judgments he has suffered from contemporary criticisms, which have given inadequate recognition to his spells as political and party manager, superior to most others. He also had a higher intellectual voltage.

The explanation is that Wilson suffered from a mental blockage when it came to imposing his leadership from above, unlike Baldwin, Attlee and Macmillan. This underlines how deep the mysteries of great leadership really lie, for Wilson was incomparably a quicker and cleverer operator in party politics than the three just mentioned. He suffered from a sense of insecurity, forever counting heads to be on the safe side. This was sad, because he nullified his considerable qualities and the great potential he possessed as the most professional of leaders. The challenge of power changed his personality of leadership. He started out with abundant courage, but it became sapped by constant tension. Vision in turn became foreshortened. On the other hand Baldwin, Attlee and Macmillan knew precisely the type of country and society they wanted to create for the future.

Wilson's perspective in similar circumstances was limited to a slot in a TV news bulletin the same evening and the impact of tomorrow's newspaper headlines the next morning. This explains why no one is ever likely to write about the Wilson Age. He did not leave the stamp of leadership on the sixties and seventies as Baldwin did on the twenties and thirties, Attlee on the 1945–51 revolution and Macmillan on the mood of the late fifties and early sixties.

If Harold Wilson funked imposing his leadership and authority, his successor James Callaghan confounded all his critics by the impressive stature he quickly acquired when he became PM. He went about his job with courage, ruthlessness and deep cunning. The Crossman Diaries gave a depressing picture of Callaghan as Chancellor in the early years of the Wilson Government, 1964–70, a scared Minister, with bowed head, forever losing his shattered nerves. To his credit Crossman revised these harsh judgments. By 1970 he was writing of 'Big Jim' with enthusiastic admiration; he 'never allows himself to be panicked . . . not just of professional political skill but of iron nerves . . . he is a master of the plain man's presentation of complex issues to which university-trained colleagues aspire and which they rarely achieve.'*

This aspect of the Personality of Leadership is relevant. I recall asking

* Profile in *New Statesman*.

13

Hugh Gaitskell, then Labour's leader, why he esteemed Callaghan's abilities so highly, in preference to his Oxbridge-shaped colleagues. Gaitskell told me that even if his mind were untrained in the academic sense, Callaghan's judgment, instinct and understanding of detailed policies was superior to that of the others who could never rival his 'feel' for the gut reaction of working people, and his understanding of what the Labour movement is all about. Close on fifteen years later Gaitskell's vision and assessment of the rival personalities of potential leadership were confirmed when Callaghan was elected leader in preference to the media's Oxonian favourites like Roy Jenkins, Denis Healey, Tony Crosland and Wedgwood Benn. Certainly Callaghan displayed the highest qualities of courage when he defied the Labour Party conference and the trade unions on his anti-inflation and wage-restraint policies, in October 1978, instead of trying to cobble meaningless compromises for the sake of peace. Along with courage he exhibited ruthlessness, even short-tempered bullying tactics, when dealing with difficult colleagues like Benn.

ART OF MAN MANAGEMENT

In the elusive art of managing men, which lies at the heart of leadership, Attlee was outstanding. This test does not rest merely on the personality to dominate and overpower Ministers, in the sense that Neville Chamberlain and Edward Heath achieved with dictatorial intolerance of views contrary to their own; but in the sense of ensuring the maximum efficiency and co-operation from all Ministers, each requiring separate understanding and subtlety in touch. This flair has nothing to do with the personality of the Prime Minister, for Attlee had none, nor of charisma for colleagues and public opinion on the national screen, for he had no sympathy for the word unless the charismatic clue cropped up in a *Times* crossword clue. But in crisp, businesslike, tough management in running Cabinets he was the master. Here I invoke the testimony of Tory and Liberal Ministers in Churchill's war-time Government. As Deputy Prime Minister Attlee frequently chaired Cabinets in Winston's absence, and was the permanent chairman of a network of Cabinet Committees. Tory Ministers like Lord Swinton, 'Rab' Butler, and Harold Macmillan, Liberal leader Sir Archibald Sinclair (the first Lord Thurso), and a massive independent like Sir John Anderson (Lord Waverley) all told me how powerful a chairman Attlee proved. His flair lay in keeping discussion flowing, getting business through, cruelly silencing long-winded Ministers. ('You've said that already'; 'No need to repeat what's in the circulated Cabinet papers'; 'Nothing more to say, I hope? Good.') His decisions were always clear-cut and emphatic. This was how a Conservative Cabinet Minister saw the two styles of management at the centre. 'Well, when

Attlee takes the chair, Cabinet meetings are businesslike and efficient; we keep to the agenda, make decisions, and get away in reasonable time. When Churchill presides, nothing is decided; we listen enthralled and go home, many hours late, feeling we have been present at an historic occasion.'* Attlee was the commonsensical common man writ uncommonly large.

Ramsay MacDonald also proved himself an excellent chairman of Cabinet and its Committees. Here, too, it is wise to be guided by the judgments of Ministers predisposed to be critical. In the National Government, when he had to balance Ministers from three parties basically hostile to each other, MacDonald, in the judgment of Tory and Liberal members of the Cabinet, proved for several years a powerful chairman until his physical and mental resources cracked under the strain of overwork. He read every Cabinet paper in circulation, all Departmental documents sent up to No 10 Downing Street. In the end he wrecked his eyesight too. He had not mastered Churchill's skill in discouraging voluminous minute-writing: 'Please explain, on one sheet of paper please, why. . . .'

If the surprise outsiders who became the unexpected Prime Ministers proved to be the greatest successes in the exercise of power once they had acquired it, what of those who were universally but prematurely acclaimed as 'the greatest' on taking office, yet proved failures? The moral after seeing so many Prime Ministers come and go is emphatic: always beware of the loud hosannus raised to heaven about the great leadership vouchsafed us by destiny and about to inspire the nation to new glories and horizons! The poor fellows never lived up to their advance billing, they ended up broken-hearted failures. In my gallery of PMs the true successes were those who represented and captured the moods and needs of their times, as sensed instinctively by the mass of the nation but seldom accepted by the fashionable opinion-formers overburdened by too much theory of power but not its practice. These tests have little to do with history's popular tests of statesmanship and greatness. Lloyd George and Churchill were hopeless as peace-time Premiers and leaders. Winston was the poorest Opposition leader I have seen, and when he became Prime Minister again in 1951 he had scant understanding of and less sympathy for the new world bequeathed him by Attlee, a national mood created by the war.

Lord Beaverbrook, writing as an insider who knew all the famous men in the first half of this century, counselled: '. . . Often what seems to be made of marble and bronze turns out, in a little, to be composed of lath and plaster.'† So it was with Neville Chamberlain and Anthony Eden.

* London Diary, *New Statesman*, August 1945.

† *Decline and Fall of Lloyd George*, Lord Beaverbrook (Collins).

Both ended their Premierships tragic, broken men. In the Anatomy of Power they possessed none of the essential qualities. The experience has nothing to do with any theory that they must have been of one type incapable of ever attaining greatness. They were opposites. Chamberlain when he got power, but not before, was the most obstinate and intolerant of all the Prime Ministers I've known. But he had great courage. In the hour of *his* challenge Eden's nerve cracked, his courage snapped. But he never did have moral and political courage, or, in human terms, guts. If he had had real moral courage, twenty years before Suez he would instantly have aligned himself with Churchill on resigning as Foreign Secretary from Chamberlain's Government, but he funked doing so because of his timidity over party unity.

It is difficult for later generations, brought up in the glow of Churchill's greatness, to realise that if Eden had been equipped with classic leadership qualities like moral courage, driving ambition for the glittering prizes, ruthlessness and cruelty, he and not Winston would have become Prime Minister when Chamberlain fell. Beaverbrook told Eden that if he had played his cards ambitiously he could have taken power. Only five months before the outbreak of war in 1939 the *News-Chronicle* published a poll of Government supporters which showed that Eden was the overwhelming favourite as Chamberlain's successor: he had five times the support of his nearest rival and had more massive support than all the other rivals added together. But he threw away all his prospects. Perhaps he lacked the necessary cold steel and passion. This might explain the Suez tragedy, too.

AGONIES OF PUBLIC LIFE

At the end of the day Chamberlain and Eden personified the intolerable and merciless cruelty of public life when the success totems are denied. Both suffered the most sickening tribal agony and sacrifice I witnessed in Parliament over nearly five decades. They were the victims of the most excruciating public crucifixion. It is a frightening sight when MPs of all parties bay like jungle beasts for the kill, primitive and merciless. Ramsay MacDonald was the third of the twelve Premiers I knew well to share this agony in his final months. They were all obviously gravely ill, shadows of their former selves, broken in the service of their country. Yet they were hounded and destroyed with unbelievable ferocity and animal-like savagery. No one spared a memory for their years of glory, when they had been cheered, idolised, and courted. MPs de-humanised themselves by such primitive behaviour, for it was impossible at the time of each to imagine any other group of people exhibiting such cruelty to their leaders, with no trace of sympathy or understanding. The tragedy of leadership is too often ignored in the 'accursed trade of politics'. It is strange that the Mother of Parliaments, the most civilised democratic assembly in the world, should show such fury and hatred without trace of mercy when Prime Ministers are offered in tribal sacrifice to the political gods at high noon. Chamberlain himself said: 'Not one shows the slightest sign of sympathy for the man or even any comprehension that there may be a human tragedy in the background.' MPs have previously been described as becoming like crabs, devouring the sick, wounded and dying among their own species.

STYLE MAKETH PREMIERS

Whereas courage, ruthlessness and other features of leadership can be superimposed and simulated, style is the most individual quality in the Anatomy of Power. With it must go standards and character to form the true Personality of Style. This is the most elusive asset to capture. Lloyd George had the most electrifying personality of all the great men I knew, but because of the cynical manner in which he exploited the honours system and his narrow squeaks over the Marconi and other scandals he fell down on standards. This explains why Stanley Baldwin was the nation's ideal Prime Minister and leader over the next fifteen years because he was identified with the people's instinct for high standards of conduct and honesty. Baldwin was accorded this recognition because he cleaned out the stables and removed the stench.

There appears to be a natural law of politics which sets an automatic rhythm of change and contrast, illustrated in particular by style and personality. The historic majesty of that other warrior-statesman, Winston Churchill, was replaced by the carefully played-down anonymity of Clement Attlee; whereas Churchill overplayed many situations and orations unnecessarily, Attlee had a genius for underplaying every big occasion by deliberately low-key performances. Anthony Eden, who made himself a nervous wreck, was replaced by the unflappable actor-manager Harold Macmillan; Sir Alec Douglas-Home, almost certain to be the last of the gentlemen players from Lord's (he did play for Middlesex) to occupy No. 10, was hustled off the scene to make way for Edward Heath, the first of a new Tory breed, the grammar-school boy from the lower middle class, personifying the abrasive pace-setting success symbols. Then after Harold Wilson, with his breathless, instant-Government reaction and gimmickry to keep the media happy, combined with the sadness of his insensitive use of the honours system to ennoble some odd characters, national opinion responded with relief to the solid four-square style of James Callaghan, who, with a sure instinct, almost like Baldwin's, set about re-establishing standards by perfecting his personal style as that of the family solicitor and family doctor, a man of honour dedicated to standards and principle. It was good type-casting. Wilson's reputation by contrast suffered. He had little sense of style. His farewell Honours List left permanent scars. He forgot the discretion applied by Balfour over a half-a-century before when the Tory leader advised the Palace on a queried recommendation: 'But though the Order of Merit would add to his reputation I do not think he would add to the reputation of the O.M.'

From these examples covering the last half-century it is obvious that there is no set mould of leadership to guarantee success. One's experience of power as it is being acted at the time, and not reconstructed generations later from yellowing pages of old minutes and diaries, confirms that really great and outstanding Premiers come every twenty to thirty years. Lloyd George and Churchill are bracketed together in historic greatness. And Baldwin, Attlee and Macmillan must be recognised as the outstanding peace-time Premiers of this century, not least because they identified with and were the symbolic leaderships of the spirit and mood of their times. Baldwin pre-eminently represented the spirit of his time, after the exhaustions of the First World War. Attlee was the medium for the determined mood of the British people for major change, reconstruction and social revolution after the Second World War. And Macmillan led and expressed the mood of the new world of the late fifties and early sixties after the post-war tumult and upheaval of the forties and fifties, as the nation sounded the last trumpet for the departed grandeur of Empire and groped towards a new niche in Europe, seeking a new role for the last third of the twentieth century.

LLOYD GEORGE AND CHURCHILL

As one of the few newsmen still around who knew and observed both Lloyd George and Winston Churchill whilst at their full vigour I am left with the impression that the country, now bereft of Empire and world status, is unlikely to be able to reproduce such leaders of genius until next century. Comparisons between them are endless. Lloyd George was by far the greater orator, the greatest master in this century of the spoken word—a quality in mass communication which has been largely destroyed in the television age when image is everything as opposed to ideas and ideals and how they are expressed. L.G. considered oratory the queen of the arts, and on the platform he had no equal; he recognised it 'as the art of swaying public opinion by speech, the essential handmaiden of democracy'. But Churchill's speeches will be read longer because they were written as great prose and declaimed as history. L.G. was a superb politician who could captivate a nation by his brilliance and charm, Churchill was the greater statesman. Lloyd George responded to people, not policies, and hated being alone. He was a magnificent listener, as I remember, forever asking questions and responding to them. Churchill brooded on history and events but not people, preferred to work with a small group whom he knew and loved, and invariably dwelt in monologues, throwing out endless ideas. Lloyd George possessed an exhilarating zest for the political manipulation of power, which often led him to cut corners. This explains the barbed comment of Sir Colin Coote, the distinguished editor of the *Daily Telegraph*, that he was uncertain whether L.G. was the greatest Prime Minister who became a cad or the greatest cad who ever became the great Prime Minister.

They were the great stylists, not only in the care they devoted to their classic oratory, its phrasing, balance, and beauty of the spoken word, but in the more human tricks of the market place. Long before Madison Avenue moved in, Lloyd George and Churchill pioneered the personality of power by providing their individualistic identities and touches. L. G's flowing hair, the shepherd's flowing cloak of the hills, the crook, as well as the eye-glasses of the period on a long silk ribbon which he used as a prop. Winston's repertoire of stylish supports was endless: his painting achievements, his brick-laying hobbies and application to the union to join as a craftsman, hats galore, the inevitable cigar, the bow tie, the walking stick, the war-time siren suit. Compared with the greats the moderns appear naked.

Standards and conduct are linked with style. Here the warrior-statesmen were unalike, and one is not thinking of Asquith's aphorism 'Lloyd George has no principles and Churchill no convictions', but in their attitude to moral judgments. Lord Beaverbrook, who worked closely with both in the two world wars, saw the contrasts in this way: 'Churchill resents an assault on his public policy as much as L. G. does an attack on his private life.' Churchill had a very thin skin, Lloyd George never minded attacks, indeed they stimulated him. Baldwin loved telling the story of how he met Lloyd George one day as a Select Committee's report was due clearing him of charges of unparliamentary conduct. He said to L.G. that the Tories had been trying for years to catch him out telling lies, and now they thought they had got him. 'They will find out this afternoon they have caught you telling the truth. They will have the shock of their lives.' Lloyd George enjoyed telling the story how he had been found out telling the truth. 'Poor old Bonar (Law), he doesn't like being called a liar. I don't mind it. I've been called a liar all my life. I've had more of the rough and tumble of life than he's had.'

THE GRAND MANNER
The Prime Minister who reintroduced style in the grand manner to catch

19

the modern instant demands of television was Harold Macmillan. He was first to realise that the modern world of communications requires the style of the theatre. The grand Edwardian manner, mixed with stylised speech adapted adroitly to the setting of the hour, on one occasion exploiting the air of effortless superiority and the longueur, the next flinging around the phrases of the street corner ('You've never had it so good') and of the race-track ('He's a ringer'). There was no mystery. The varieties of style reflected the multitude of contradictions in temperament and personality of a highly-strung, introspective, tough political cunning, and the high scholarship of his Balliol distinctions. In Macmillan's case, the Prime Minister was many men. He gloried in the benefits which the affluent society brought to the lowest-paid workers whom he identified with his 'Stockton'* conscience—even though he was criticised for creating the candy-floss society. He wanted his style to be associated with affluent expansion, not depression.

In the exploitation of style and personality Ramsay MacDonald succeeded in providing the impact of glamour and romance to leadership. His was an imposing and impressive figure, handsome—'a Prince among men', to quote Lord Shinwell who knew all the big personalities of the century—and he was a master in using his attractive voice like an organ. Style was even more important in his case, because Labour, struggling to break through, required inspiration, vision and idealism—and he was inspiring. It was the time when eyes had to be lifted to the hills; his style matched the hour. In his case, the myth created over his final National Government days distorted the real man and his place as one of the makers of the twentieth century. His greatest value in leadership, at his particular moment in history, was that he gave the emerging Labour movement that unusual political quality of 'soul' which lost its appeal under more colourless leaders overwhelmed by instant economic problems of today with no time left for the soul and the vision.

Style so far has been seen in terms of the sweeping gesture, the dramatic entrance, the flair for histrionic glamour in the spotlight. But style can be equally powerful when it exploits non-style. Nobody could have had a firmer grip on the affections and loyalties of the mass of the people than Clement Attlee, yet no Prime Minister has been duller in personality or less inspiring in his public exercises; the impact of his de-stylised manner was due to the fact that people could identify with what he achieved in post-war reconstruction. This achievement was much subtler in execution than say the inspirational identity achieved by Lloyd George and Churchill. Attlee's style created a rapport with the working classes of unselfconscious naturalness that is not often found at the disposal of

* Harold Macmillan's first Parliamentary seat was Stockton-on-Tees.

middle-class leaders. He exhibited all the qualities of the common man to an uncommon degree.

James Callaghan stylised himself deliberately as the reassuring family doctor and legal adviser, without ever trying to put on the polished refinements of the Harley Street consultant or the advocate specialising in the higher skills of corporation lawyers. This concentration upon the plain man's personality was similar to Baldwin's profile. Pehaps that explains why Callaghan, an elementary and secondary-school boy, saw off four double-firsts from Oxford when he won the leadership. The chaps preferred the homespun understanding of the shop floor to the talk at high table. This was part of the secret of style. He concentrated upon the plain man's guide to politics and the realities of power. But behind this clever 'You Can Trust Jim' front he was cunning, ruthless, adroit—as all the best Premiers have been—identifying more naturally with Attlee than with Wilson and, appropriate for a radical conservative with a small 'c', with Tory leaders in the tradition of Baldwin and Macmillan. For that basically is what politics is about: the battle for the centre.

But in the manner of leading their Governments and parties all the Prime Ministers have shared a faculty common to all, so prevalent indeed as to become a conditioned reflex. This styling refers to the endless U-turns which they have all performed, reconciling high principles, without too much agony of conscience, with cynical expediency. Harold Wilson suffered heavily at the hands of critics for constantly somersaulting in policies, notably over the plans to impose legal disciplines on trade unions known as the 'In Place of Strife' crisis. He suffered excessively, I felt, because of a central weakness in his style: his inability ever to admit he was wrong and to represent all defeats as grand victories. If he had only studied Baldwin's reassuring techniques many of the wounds suffered from attacks on his political character would never have occurred. Baldwin excelled in frankness; to Churchill's chagrin, his 'frank avowal of error'* always ensured forgiveness for Baldwin.

Wilson was only one among many, though others were cleverer in concealing the swing. For sheer smooth professionalism in style of changing course, without worrying the passengers too much by telling them that his new compass reading compelled the captain to steer for new ports, Harold Macmillan was the master. In more than one major issue he made turns of 180 degrees, considerably more startling than the credulity of parties and electors is normally expected to tolerate, and got away with it. When they preferred Macmillan over Butler to succeed Eden the Tories, in their Suez mood, were convinced that they had rightly insisted on and got a Right-winger for the leadership. By very controlled and subtle leadership

*The Gathering Storm, Winston S. Churchill (Cassell).

he hauled down the old Imperial flag all over Africa and elsewhere, he liquidated Empire almost everywhere, he made entry to Europe acceptable and inevitable; and if Jim Callaghan became later the most conservative leader imaginable for the Labour Party in reassuring the City, boardroom, and managements that he meant no ill, Harold Macmillan proved the most radical and socialistic PM of the Tory Party measured by social change in mass working-class standards. Under Macmillan many of the old Tory skins were sloughed off painlessly, without the creature feeling a thing. That's style. Even Churchill had to change course to keep afloat in the storm-tides of history. He said he had not become Prime Minister in order to preside over the liquidation of the British Empire. By the time he retired the Empire which he so loved was departing for ever.

These constant changes in course, when the sacred scrolls of election manifestos have to be scrapped, come to all Prime Ministers. The experience of doing precisely the opposite of what was promised has become an inexorable law of politics and power. The dilemma is how to reconcile the clash between high political principle and idealism and low political compromise and cunning. All PMs are soon ensnared in the trap. The differences between them are found in style. Harold Macmillan and James Callaghan effected the changes in the relaxed smoothness of confidence. Harold Wilson and Edward Heath did their somersaults in the breathless heat of panic.

THE PEACEFUL REVOLUTION
The real significance of Attlee and Macmillan is too often overlooked by the academics. They formed a unique duo among the Prime Ministers. They provided the bridges linking the between-the-wars and pre-1914 worlds of the British Empire on the one hand and the world left over after 1945. Whereas Winston Churchill was totally out of sympathy with the second half of the twentieth century, Attlee and Macmillan between them masterminded the two crucial interlocking stages in Britain's evolution to the world of today. Macmillan's triumph was in lining up the Conservative Party to a new post-Imperial destiny without party upheaval, Attlee's by imposing his personality and style of leadership on a party normally convulsed with the urge for regicide and suicide, to go straight through for a massive peaceful revolution in social, human and industrial priorities.

By comparison with Macmillan's studied style in making the Tory Party change course and beliefs, Edward Heath's authoritarian methods to compel the party to make many U-turns on wages, prices and inflation proved disastrous for the party. Style provides the secret. Heath's bustling, abrasive, challenging, go-getting approach may be excellent for entrepreneurs, but for dealing with people in the Tory mass the quiet, relaxed, skilful flairs of Macmillan and Baldwin provided the success stories history. But underneath the style, which so often concealed the more brilliant arts of statecraft, they were cunning, adroit and cruel, the indispensable qualities in leadership. Heath, by comparison, had little patience and less tolerance when he became PM, when his character, I remain convinced, underwent a metamorphosis. Otherwise I am sure he would have proved a great radical leader. As Richard Crossman saw him: 'the cutting edge of his intellectual honesty is only matched by the bluntness of his intuition.'

After over thirty years in Parliament Macmillan's feel for history told him the importance of style and tone. Within hours of succeeding Eden he grabbed his Chief Whip, Edward Heath, and announced: 'We're off to the Turf to celebrate with champagne and oysters.' Which struck the right note in the depressing situation he inherited; people preferred the gaiety of spirit to any sombre soliloquy on the doorstep of No. 10 about how inadequate he felt to cope with such herculean problems awaiting him inside. And next morning his first act on taking over was to pin the following quotation from Gilbert and Sullivan on the connecting door leading to the staff offices: 'Calm deliberation unravels every knot.' A shrewd move to bring down the high fevers which ran under Eden. The two incidents set the style and tone for his Premiership until he started losing his touch and luck began, as always, running against him six years later.

CRUELTY OF POWER

While courage, patience, vision, judgment and the other abiding verities of leadership are allotted to Prime Ministers in varying degrees, it is surprising to find that cruelty and ruthlessness, alas, are such greatly esteemed qualities in the personality of leadership. All the textbooks on power claim that to be a good butcher is one of the chief qualities of power. This is not merely an academic judgment. Those who live closest to the centre—Cabinet Secretaries, Permanent Secretaries, and the select groups of advisers all Premiers gather around them—place the highest premium of all on ruthlessness. Their reasons for this, I found, derive from the very nature of the office. The Prime Minister holds the loneliest job of all. There are no friendships at the top. The phrase, I should record, was wryly used by Churchill to 'Rab' Butler, who suffered more than most from the odd values on loyalty and friendship politicians profess when power is up for grabs. Leaders have to walk alone. As Baldwin wrote to Asquith when he left the House of Commons: 'I don't think that anyone who has not been a Prime Minister can realise the essential and ultimate loneliness of that position, there is no veil between him and the

23

human heart.' And Asquith brooded on the 'unsharable solitude' of the job. Whether the loneliness and isolation roughens character and eliminates the quality of mercy, or whether the position merely sharpens the zest for survival and self-preservation as a primeval inhumanity cannot be actuarily balanced, but the fact remains that all the Prime Ministers I have known have never exhibited any squeamishness in their butchery or been sickened by the sight of blood—providing it is other people's.

Lloyd George was inhuman by the unfeeling way in which he could throw out Ministers, colleagues and staff when they were no longer of use to him. Honours, titles, ribbons, patronage, he sprayed around him as from a hose-pipe, but invariably to those on their way up with service of value to render the great man, but seldom to those he decided to discard after years of devotion. Sir Arthur Salter, who as a top civil servant and Minister knew him well, wrote that L. G. 'showed little mercy to those who were broken in his service' and that he possessed 'a kind of animal revulsion from a sick member of the herd'.* He was inhuman in his detachment when colleagues were in trouble. Winston Churchill often showed a streak of cruelty, in the opinion of Robert Boothby (later Lord Boothby), who was his Parliamentary Private Secretary as early as 1926 and was one of the only four friends who formed the Churchill group in the pre-war years. Winston would pick up and drop men at will, according to their usefulness to him at the moment. Indeed, Boothby told me that Sir Oswald Mosley, before he became leader of the British Union of Fascists, advised him against seeing too much of Churchill because he 'would not allow criticism, which he saw as betrayal and disloyalty, but demanded total loyalty'.

But Churchill was too emotional and warm-hearted a man to be deliberately cruel and cause injury to the feelings of old friends. He could never be vindictive or bear grudges. He could be as ruthless as any in the pursuit of ambition and power, but he was magnanimous without fail in victory. Despite the tragedy of appeasement and his own isolation in the inter-war years, he treated Neville Chamberlain with conspicuous generosity of spirit when he became Prime Minister, despite the political pressures on him to throw Chamberlain to the wolves. And when the rejected Premier died of cancer a few months later, Winston was in tears as he cried that he did not know what he would do without him: 'I was counting on dear Neville to run the home front for me.' For such a war lord, he had a soft heart; he cried unashamedly over deaths of friends—and his pets. James Stuart (later Viscount Stuart of Findhorn), when he was Chief Whip in Churchill's Government, frequently told me of his difficulty in persuading Winston to sack a Minister even when it was patently overdue. He

* *Personality in Politics*, J. A. Salter.

would resist for months, and then cry: 'It's a shame. You made me do it!'* Magnanimity was his most personal quality.

Baldwin, by comparison, exhibited much more ruthless calculation when he came to power. In 1935 he dropped Sir Samuel Hoare, his Foreign Secretary, without much conscience, when he realised that the Hoare-Laval pact to pacify Mussolini over his invasion of Abyssinia was unpopular; he destroyed Lloyd George, whom he detested, and disdained the Press Lords, Beaverbrook and Rothermere. Neville Chamberlain, much more autocratic in human relations, never attempted to conceal his contempt and ruthlessness when dealing with his critics; even top men in the Civil Service and Foreign Office were kicked around so that he could hand-pick senior advisers who enthusiastically supported his appeasement policies and initiatives.

Surprisingly, the 'meek little mouse' Clement Attlee proved about the toughest and most unfeeling of all, without ever appearing to be sorry when despatching old and trusted colleagues to the knackers yard. He went on record with the opinion that ruthlessness was the most essential quality in a Premier. He practised his beliefs with cold detachment. Early on during his post-war Government Richard Crossman discovered the streak of cruelty in his leader's make-up which seemed so out of character. Attlee dismissed Ministers with colder, sharper steel than deployed by any other Premier, showing a callous indifference to the shock and injured feelings of his victims. This streak of heartlessness was pronounced in most of his personal dealings, although in other respects he was dedicated to maintaining standards of public conduct. I recall the peremptory even inhuman way in which he sacked a Scottish Secretary friend of mine who had been very close to the leader for twenty years. Attlee summoned him one day to No. 10 Downing Street. In the Cabinet room Attlee got down to business without ceremony.

'Good t'see you. I'm carrying through Government changes. Want your job for somebody else. Sake of the party, y'know. Write me the usual letter. Think of something as the excuse. Health, family, too much travelling, constituency calls. Anything will do. Good fellow. Thanks.'

It was all over. No routine civilities. No bromides. No hope of another job. No peerage with a Lords office dangled temptingly. The axe had fallen. That was that.

The Minister suddenly realised he had been sacked, with naked brutality. He gathered his second wind. 'But why, Prime Minister? Why have you sacked me like this, without warning, with no complaints that I know of, no talk in advance?'

Removing his pipe from his mouth, looking up from the papers on which

* *Within the Fringe*, Viscount Stuart (Bodley Head).

he had re-started to write, Attlee barked: ''Cos you don't measure up to yer job. That's why. Thanks for coming. Secretary will show you out.'

That was the exit, the kill: clean, sharp, no delay. They had been close buddies and comrades together at Westminster for twenty years. A Prime Minister, in Attlee's judgment, cannot afford to be chicken-hearted even with friends of a life-time. Attlee could justify or rationalise this unfeeling butchery of an old and dear friend by the verdict: 'It's awkward to sack a man. But tell him if he doesn't make the grade. It's not playing straight with the fellow to pretend you'll try to fit him into another slot.' That was how he rationalised all his sackings.

But for massacre in style, on the grand scale, Harold Macmillan was the grandmaster among all the pastmasters. In a notorious night of the long knives he despatched seven Cabinet Ministers in one exercise. With the Tory Party and public opinion highly critical of his Government and its policies, morale was alarmingly low and in a state of panic after a series of shockingly bad by-election defeats. So Macmillan, his Premiership obviously under dangerous strain, decided to carry through a massive Government purge. In the process he threw out seven very close colleagues and friends, as well as others further down the pecking order. The exercise inflicted severe injury to his reputation, and at the same time destroyed his image of unflappable leadership. This was not a putsch to liquidate dangerous rivals planning a power coup to overthrow him. Instead, it was activated in panic to save his own skin. Viscount Kilmuir, the Lord Chancellor and Macmillan's closest friend among the seven victims, re-created the scene in the Cabinet room when he was sent for at short notice and told to pack his bags: 'I got the impression that the Prime Minister was extremely alarmed about his own position and was determined to eliminate any risk for himself by a massive change of Government.'* In this case there was the added irony that Kilmuir had boasted shortly before that 'loyalty is the Tories' secret weapon.'

This 'Glencoe massacre' coming several years after he had become Prime Minister sharpens the moral drawn later in this chapter about how even the best Prime Ministers start losing their touch after they have been too long in power. The butchery was carried through by a desperate Prime Minister whose nerves had been shot to pieces, whereas earlier he had coped with major resignations with superior style and assumed disdain. He mocked the resignation of his entire Treasury team of three, headed by his Chancellor, Peter Thorneycroft, as 'a little local difficulty' and flew off next morning on his Commonwealth tour. When the Marquis of Salisbury resigned from his Cabinet in protest at the Government's decision to release President Makarios and allow him to return to Cyprus,

* *Political Adventure*, Lord Kilmuir (Weidenfeld & Nicolson).

26

he commented that less notice was paid than he expected. Nigel Birch (later Lord Rhyl), who had earlier resigned with the Thorneycroft team—Enoch Powell was the third—and was a persistent critic, threw the most poisonous barb. The day after the massacre of the seven, he solemnly rose in the Commons to congratulate Mr Macmillan on keeping his head when all about him were losing theirs.

Although Harold Wilson modelled himself on Harold Macmillan's style—he genuinely admired the Conservative leader—he stopped short in following the lead as a butcher. He probably erred on the soft side. By sacking a man, Wilson reasoned, a Prime Minister gratuitously makes twenty enemies: the fellow who is sacked and the nineteen others who believe they have a prior claim to the vacant office. He was a kind and sympathetic man at heart, predisposed to bend over backwards to excuse errors of judgment by friends—a generosity of mind which contributed eventually to the troubles in his 'kitchen Cabinet'.

Whereas Attlee carved out a special role for himself as a former Prime Minister and became canonised in Labour's history with affection bordering on adoration, Harold Wilson's retirement did not engender much enthusiasm for him in the memory of his party. This was another example of the cruelty of public life and the ingratitude of politics. Perhaps he would have been wiser if he had followed Harold Macmillan's advice about not hanging around the green room when you retire after having played the great roles in the grand theatre of politics. The American tradition for ex-Presidents to quit Washington and return to their roots in their home states works out more kindly in the end. Wilson suffered painfully in reputation because by hanging around the scene he became involved in irrelevant and trivial controversies. He was much bigger a man than he allowed himself to be.

VISION AND IDEALS

Of the fifty Prime Ministers from Sir Robert Walpole to James Callaghan those who left the greatest impact on history were inspired by vision and ideals, who pursued their dreams until they were realised. Vision is an elusive, almost metaphysical quality in leadership. Premiers with luck can get by when selecting the right decisions of the varied alternatives put before them; they can survive for a long time by shrewd management of Cabinets, parties and Parliament; by butchery of near and dear colleagues without shedding a tear about the gory sight. But without vision and the inspiration of new frontiers and beckoning horizons they will soon be forgotten, however good they were as administrators, technocrats, managers, fixers and power manipulators. By contrast, the most inspiring PMs have been those gifted with a flair to lift people's eyes to the future,

with ideals worth achieving. It is given to few to create this uplift of spirituality.

Of the Prime Ministers in this portrait gallery the greatest were most
inspired by vision and idealism. When he was in his eighties Lloyd George
was asked what was his proudest achievement in his long life. He did not
reply, as history might expect, that it was his inspiring and victorious
leadership in the First World War which saved Britain and the Western
world from catastrophic defeat by German militarism. Instead, in his own
level of human values, he was proudest of introducing the first versions of
the national health service and social security which rescued masses of
people from hardship, starvation and other affronts to human dignity by
a State that cared. In 1911 this was how he saw his vision: 'At no distant
date I hope that the State will acknowledge full responsibility for making
provision for sickness, breakdown, and unemployment . . . Poor Law
systems have been so harsh and humiliating that working-class pride
revolts against accepting so degrading and doubtful a boon . . . the obli-
gation of the State to find labour or sustenance will be realised.' At the
end of the journey his greatest pride was his social justice programme
rather than his achievements as a war leader responsible for the overthrow of the Kaiser.

Whereas Lloyd George was inspired by vision in terms of human
beings, Winston Churchill, by comparison, saw the future in power
terms, measured by the grandeur and glory of power and dominion.
Indeed, in many ways Neville Chamberlain displayed a more realistic
foresight about the future condition of the Western world than Churchill.
He was gripped in his appeasement policies by the fear of Communism
engulfing European civilisation and that a Second World War would
destroy the British Empire. His foresight was clearer than Churchill's.
Winston at the end of the war believed that Imperial greatness would continue for generations; and only started to make speeches about the Communist menace after the doctrine of unconditional surrender (in company
with President Roosevelt) made certain of not only the destruction of
Hitler and his Nazis but the dismemberment of Germany and the extension of Communist dictatorship over much of Europe.

One moral comes through quite clearly in assessing the values of vision,
for among the Prime Ministers in this study those who had the greatest
genius to inspire the vision of human happiness and social and national
well-being shared a common heritage and blood stock. Lloyd George,
Stanley Baldwin, Ramsay MacDonald and Harold Macmillan were all
Celts. To include Baldwin, seen as the Midlands ironmaster embodying
all the phlegmatic English virtues, and Macmillan, product of Eton and
Balliol, with the mannered style of the Edwardian country houses and the

world of dukes, may seem out of character. Both were Celts, I found, just as much as Lloyd George and MacDonald, even though the Hebridean blood and dreams came from a generation removed. Iain Macleod, himself a Highlander in blood and vision from the Western Isles, had no difficulty in identifying with the fellow Highlander in Baldwin. This stock, he claimed, gave Baldwin his superb gift of language and poetry through his mother's family: MacDonalds from the Isles.

Similarly, as a north-east Scot without a drop of Highland blood in my veins, I always found the Celtic strain most pronounced every time I saw Harold Macmillan privately. In all the Ministerial rooms he occupied throughout Whitehall—Housing, Local Government, Defence, Treasury, Foreign Office and, of course, No. 10—I always noticed that space was reserved, often displacing some valuable work of art from the State collections, for the picture of the modest Highland croft which his grandfather left for London to found the famous Macmillan publishing house. All this was part of the real inner man. It was not a gimmick. He in his daydreams beheld the Hebrides. He would talk endlessly and with great sensitivity to me about what the humble croft meant to him. He could identify my authentic Scottish accent with his grandfather's. To him all this represented his roots.

The point is made in order to explain the identity of style of these four Highlanders. They were the classic articulators and communicators, the idealists and the visionaries, whose oratory was invariably inspired by visions of the way ahead, not related to accountancy and the gross national product but reaching for the peaks. This was MacDonald's greatest contribution as one of the makers of the twentieth century, for he provided the ideals and dreams when they were needed most. Perhaps this is what Labour has lost and not yet re-discovered, the idealism to lift men's eyes.

Lloyd George, Baldwin, MacDonald and Macmillan were extraordinarily difficult men to understand, for they loved to withdraw themselves introspectively into their Celtic mists. Their speeches had an elusive mysticism and imagery. This intuitive feel for communicating dreams and visions was peculiar to the clan spirituality which survived time and place. This explains why Chamberlain, a better manager and administrator, lacked Baldwin's idealistic spark; why Eden and Douglas-Home were pedestrian communicators when compared with Macmillan's colour and sense of theatre; why Wilson and Callaghan have been unable to recapture MacDonald's inspirational fire. The first Lord Birkenhead sensed his indefinable something in Lloyd George's 'eerie intuition, subtlety, divination'.

The irony is that in an age which has revolutionised technical communications the capacity to inspire people's hearts and minds with new visions for their children and children's children has been the first casualty in the modern war for images and pictures and not ideals and thoughts. The new generation like Edward Heath, Harold Wilson, James Callaghan and Margaret Thatcher are in the same mould as technocrats, administrators, machine-minders who know the mechanics and the levers of the State apparatus but are without inspiration. But technocrats, however efficient, cannot see visions of the great society or the new horizons. This in turn limits the colour and variety for anyone fascinated by the personality of leadership.

Vision is the quality which distinguishes statesmen from politicians. John Morley wrote the basic text more than sixty years ago: 'Wise statesmen are those who foresee what changes time is bringing and try to shape institutions and to mould men's thoughts and purpose in accordance with the changes that are silently surrounding them.' It seemed at one time that Harold Wilson might find himself in this group of leaders with vision when he promised the white heat of the technological revolution to change society. But he lost this idealism when compelled to deploy his great skills of management to keep his Government and party in one piece. Others shared this fate of unrealised visions and objectives. One of the paradoxes of history is that Chamberlain and Churchill have been identically treated by posterity, because the former's appeasement policies and the latter's glorious war leadership were unable to prevent the destruction of what they hoped to preserve: the mighty British Empire and the sacrifice of much of Europe to Communism.

Where the men with vision differed from the technocrats and the organisation men lay in their capacity and instinct to lift people's consciousness from their primary interest in immediate material needs to the ideals of social values and moral standards: and qualities affecting society as a whole and the worth of human living. In short, they brought to politics an attitude of mind, an approach to power, which inspired men's idealism. Blood, too, comes into the qualities of greatness and statesmanship at its highest levels. This comparison between mixed ancestry and pure English blood was made by President de Gaulle to President Kennedy in discussing Britain's most famous leaders like Churchill, Lloyd George, and Disraeli, with Macmillan and Baldwin added for good measure.

REBELS AND CONFORMISTS
Another important lesson emerging from one's study of power at the centre and the varied qualities of leadership at first-hand is that the Prime Ministers who are most dedicated to party orthodoxy by training and

total loyalty by inclination invariably prove the most weak and indifferent. It is the Prime Ministers with the most mobile loyalties, who can show disenchantment with many features of their party's profiles—in short, the Cross-bench slant of mind—who are likely to prove the outstanding successes in history.

By all conceivable tests, Lloyd George and Winston Churchill had unbelievably bad track records as party men. They were both Coalitionists at heart. As early as 1910 Lloyd George, then Chancellor of the Exchequer, was pressing Asquith, his Prime Minister, that there was an overwhelming case for a merger of the Liberal and Conservative parties. His argument was in favour of the elitism of greatness: there are not more than half-a-dozen men in each party of outstanding ability and experience, he wrote to his Prime Minister. Others were second and third-raters. By then Churchill had made the first of his two spectacular breaks with the Conservatives and, at the time, adorned the illustrious pre-1914 Liberal Government. One of the conditions of the Conservatives agreeing to join Lloyd George's war-time Coalition in 1916 was that renegade Winston should be banned from holding office. Lloyd George for his part ended the First World War without a party, with the Liberals destroyed for all time. For the next twenty years, when he still dominated world politics, he survived with a family party group consisting of son and daughter. In the early twenties Churchill, with Lloyd George, Birkenhead, Carson and other famous men, tried unsuccessfully to organise a new Centre Party formed from progressive Tories, Coalition Liberals (as distinct from Asquith's 'Wee Frees'*) and the first generation of moderates then emerging in the newly formed Labour Party and the trade union leaders. They failed, because the party machines proved too strong for them. Then Churchill decided to swim for it and for a time was a Constitutionalist, as an ex-Liberal, ex-Conservative looking for landfall. Then came reconciliation with the Conservatives, to become Baldwin's Chancellor in 1924. Then another split, when he walked out of the Shadow Cabinet in 1930 over India, and found himself in quarantine with his four paladins in Parliament throughout the thirties. Then Hitler's invasion of Poland brought him back to the Conservative Government under Chamberlain. Yet his most scathing and brilliant oratory had been at the Tories' expense for most of his career.

There is no doubt that among the peace-time Prime Ministers the outstanding successes have been those who did not conceal their substantial anxieties about their parties. Baldwin was disillusioned by the intake of the new inter-war generation of Tories at Westminster. Many of the

* 'Wee Frees' were the adherents of Asquith after the Asquith-Lloyd George break-up of the Liberal Party.

types, with dubious characters, worried him. 'Hard-faced men who have done well out of the war,' was his comment as party leader. He also wrote: 'The prevailing type is a rather successful looking business kind, which is not very attractive.'

Asked one day what he would have liked to have been instead of Tory leader Premier Baldwin confessed he would have preferred to have been leader of men and women who did not belong to any party. This was not a pose. Within my own observation, he spent more time in the lobbies and tearooms at the House of Commons gossiping with the new Labour MPs, especially those from the trade unions, than with Tory MPs. This was a daily experience. Today it would be unique because party and class barriers are sadly stronger. Attlee was in no doubt: 'SB had more in common with a lot of our chaps than he had with his own crowd. He was not really a Tory at heart, y'know. He hadn't much time for them, tell you the truth.' Archbishop Lang described him 'as a man who belonged to all parties' because he represented the spirit of the nation 'which was confined to none'.

For some time I remained convinced that Edward Heath was to continue in the Baldwin-Macmillan tradition, when he tried as Prime Minister to give the Conservative Party a new direction and a classless identity. This trend was particularly notable when he was sickened by what he castigated as the 'unacceptable face of capitalism'. He obviously felt betrayed when it was discovered that, for example, one notable person had been paid some £300,000 into a private account in the Seychelles in order to avoid paying tax. Why should he expect the trade unionist on the shop floor to have a conscience over inflation and prices when he demanded a few pounds extra in his wage packet, when one man could get away with so much untaxed wealth as part of the City system? Alas, helmsman Heath lost his bearings through too many turn-arounds in policy. It did not assist the process, as *Private Eye* noted, when he honoured those whom he had previously derided.

In this respect, Macmillan was again very much like Baldwin. During the thirties he was so sickened with his own Conservative Party that he not only resigned the party whip—in effect, putting himself beyond the pale—but on the testimony of Attlee, never a romancer, he was on the point of joining the Labour Party. 'Talks were going on, I knew about them. Know what that would have meant? Macmillan would have been leader of the Labour Party, not me.'* Indeed, Macmillan had much more intimate links and sympathies with Lloyd George than he had with the Tory leaders of the period—'extinct volcanoes' as he derided them. Like Baldwin, he succeeded in carrying through many un-Conservative poli-

* *The Abuse of Power*, James Margach (W. H. Allen).

cies. Baldwin transformed his party's old Imperial mission when he first started to liquidate the Empire and create the scene for a Commonwealth-Dominion role for India. What Baldwin started Macmillan finished a quarter-century later, when he hauled down the Union Jack in Africa and elsewhere, as the 'wind of change' carried him from world outposts to cross-channel ferries to Europe.

Later on, Edward Heath caught up with the Baldwin-Macmillan tradition when he condemned the economic-wages policies of his successor, Mrs Margaret Thatcher. In due course he was the victim of attacks by the party machine for disloyalty and betrayal as a dangerous counter-revolutionary, the identical charges thrown against earlier Conservative leaders like Baldwin, Churchill and Macmillan. He is thus in good company, if he can stay the course with patience: Peel was the first to rate patience as the most precious quality of leadership when politics have to be played long, in conflict with party scrolls. Heath was as tough as they come, very authoritarian in style and manner. He showed real courage of leadership when he sacked Enoch Powell from his Shadow Cabinet for the latter's first controversial speech on race and colour instead of trying to gloss over the split in basic human policies. He showed no mealy-mouthed compromise when he condemned the 'call-girl society' in which some Tory Ministers had become involved.

By comparison, study Neville Chamberlain and Anthony Eden. They were the creations and creatures of their party. Their first loyalty was always to the party, its central organisation and its grassroots. It is strange they should be bracketed in this test of success and failure, because they had so little in common. When Eden resigned as Foreign Secretary from Chamberlain's Government, his first priority was to avoid distressing or straining Conservative unity. For this reason he deliberately kept his distance from Churchill and never identified himself with Winston's anti-Nazi campaign, not even after Munich. He never had him at the Eden group meetings in case he himself might suffer in the party's eyes, from guilt by association with infidel Churchill. Let me call Attlee as an on-the-spot witness. Labour's leader was convinced that Eden's 'softly-softly' line was due to his anxiety to keep sweet with the Tory Establishment and to get back into office as soon as might be respectable. For his part, Chamberlain saw his own role as party chairman and leader, and then Prime Minister, to treat the party machine as of paramount interest. It was impossible for him to have any rapport with Labour leaders. He could never avoid sneering and deriding Labour, never acknowledging their role in Parliament and in the country. Then he was surprised and hurt when Labour agreed to join a Coalition only on condition that he first surrender his seals of office as his contribution to national unity.

Both Chamberlain and Eden were the most intransigent and unbending party partisans on my card. Each was unceremoniously ditched by his party in the end, without thanks and with no sympathy. Whereas the prodigals returning from afar were always clasped to the Tory bosom and forgiven—and in due course canonised.

OBSTINATE OLD MEN

One of the most neglected features in studies of the anatomy and personality of leadership is the obstinacy of Prime Ministers in even considering surrendering power once they have acquired it. Despite the fact that they obviously age at twice or three times the normal rate of advancing years while they are at No. 10 Downing Street—though retirement rejuvenates them wonderfully in many cases—the majority cling like leeches to power long after it is apparent that they are past their best, fighting the inexorable process of declining physical and mental powers, pretending that they are still fit for service at the top long after they have obviously outlived their capacity. Power becomes the drug on which they are hooked. In the variety of changes advocated by reformers—a written constitution, modernising Parliament, Bill of Rights—no one has suggested a constitutional maximum tenure for the office of Prime Minister. Peel and Baldwin both said that for health reasons no one should be Prime Minister for more than five years. The time-scale is relevant. Within my own experience covering the Westminster scene and Whitehall for so long I can confirm that those who exceeded five years in the job started going into decline very rapidly, in some cases at alarming speed. There can be no doubt that the history of this country during the past fifty years would have been significantly different if Prime Ministers had accepted the inevitability of time and timed their farewells accordingly. As it was, none of them left No. 10 fit men or happy men.

This power addiction has afflicted the notably biggest statesmen in history as well as the less distinguished incumbents. Winston Churchill advised Lloyd George that he should have gone at the very peak of his fame and height of his powers, in 1918, after winning the First World War, instead of becoming embroiled in squalid electioneering and party politics for another twenty years. Alas, Churchill ignored his own advice when his turn came. He defied with anger and sometimes with childish petulance all moves and advice to persuade him to go; even some considerable time after he had suffered a series of strokes and infirmities. The giants who possessed incomparable courage and vision to save the nation and freedom in both World Wars lacked the capacity to recognise when the time had come for them to make way for new men to cope with post-war problems. Post-war reconstruction at home was boring. They could

34

only re-live their world roles and were incapable as old men of coming to terms with reality as the world moved on. Much lesser men, too, had no clue when to make their excuses and leave.

Lloyd George's determination to hold on to power at all costs after he had won the war—he did not care where he was going, someone said, so long as he was in the driving seat—had a calamitous effect upon the entire political history of the twenties and thirties. His 'coupon' election in 1918, which cashed in on loyalty and victory, followed by his bitter feud with that other great Prime Minister, Asquith, speeded the total and final disintegration of the Liberal Party, and made easier the breakthrough by Labour which in one go replaced the Liberals as the natural alternative in a two-party system. And although he remained a dominant political personality for two decades, without achieving office, he ended solely a one-man family group.

I found Winston Churchill an even sadder case. If only he had gone shortly after 1945, at the height of his fame and glory, the shadows of the final years would have been avoided. By 1947 it was all too apparent to me and my contemporaries in the Westminster lobbies that he was totally out of sympathy with the mood and the idealism of the post-war world. Clement Attlee had captured it and reflected it. Churchill could not understand it. I found many prominent Tory Shadow Ministers who had served in his war-time Government alarmed at the stance Churchill was taking. He showed only passing interest in the social and economic policies on the home front, but wanted to concentrate all his energies on foreign affairs and defence, as he had in the thirties. After his electioneering blunder in identifying his war-time Labour Ministers as seeking to introduce Gestapo methods under a Labour Government, he sneered at the nation of 'Weary Willies and Tired Tims' being created by the post-war social services. Indeed, as I reported at the time, it was this attitude which led to Iain Macleod, Edward Heath and others forming the One Nation Group in order to persuade the Tory Party to come to terms with the realities of the post-war world.

FAILING FACULTIES

This situation became so sensitive that two years after the War a group of senior Conservative Shadow Cabinet Ministers met in secret at the London home of Captain Harry Crookshank (later Lord Crookshank) when it was unanimously decided that Churchill must be firmly told that it was time for him to retire gracefully and make way for a new leader. James Stuart, as Chief Conservative Whip, tells in his memoirs,* how he was given the disagreeable task of telling Winston of the state of party

* *Within the Fringe*, Viscount Stuart (Bodley Head).

opinion in favour of his farewell. Stuart does not quote the actual words, but Churchill obviously exploded in anger. He refused to go, or even consider going. That was in 1947. It was defiance by an old man on the grand scale. He did not finally retire until 1955. In between, he became Prime Minister once again, for four more years, and suffered a series of incapacitating strokes which were kept secret. Even when it was obvious that he was in sad decline he still held on, obstinately refusing to go with dignity. In his later stages as Prime Minister he preferred playing his favourite game of bezique to dealing with State documents. It was a painful twilight for the great man. Quite apart from politics, powerful personalities above the battle, like Lord Montgomery of Alamein, were convinced that Winston should never have become Prime Minister in 1951—he was then several years older than Lloyd George was when he had advised him to retire.

If Winston Churchill had only been persuaded to go full of honours shortly after 1945, Anthony Eden would have become Prime Minister in 1951, when he was a much fitter all-round man than he was four years later when he took over. This was Eden's tragedy, because with a longer continuous experience as Prime Minister he might have avoided the catastrophe of Suez in 1956, if indeed the crisis had emerged on the same scale under a Prime Minister who had been in undisputed control for the first half of the fifties.

Clement Attlee repeated the identical misjudgments of Winston Churchill in timing his retirement. He had been Deputy Prime Minister in the war-time Coalition of 1940–45. Then he had been Prime Minister through 1945–51. He had thus been at the top for eleven exhausting years of unrelieved pressure, and was Opposition leader in the pre-war crisis years. It was painfully clear to me that after such a continuous strain he was fading fast, his flair for leadership and judgment weakening. In five years he had carried through a massive economic, social and industrial revolution. This left him depleted, but he proved an obstinate man. Because he was over the top his mis-timing of two general elections proved disastrous for Labour. He rushed the general election for February 1950 instead of waiting for early summer, because Cripps, as Chancellor, could not compromise his high principles by a Budget in April which might be criticised as too popular for electioneering purposes.

Then in 1951, with a majority of five, he rushed another election against the advice of his party professionals. If the stamina of an overtired man had not already gone, he would not have made such costly miscalculations. If he had retired in 1950 and made way for Herbert Morrison, and given Aneurin Bevan the Foreign Office when Ernest Bevin died, Labour would have got its second wind for the fifties and avoided the internal strife which tormented it for the next two decades. The final stages of

Attlee's Premiership, like Churchill's and Macmillan's, showed how old men, after savouring the delights of power for too long, become more obstinate and reluctant to go, as well as suffer the enfeebling weaknesses of age advancing at double the normal pace.

But defeat in 1951 did not close the Attlee story. He held on as Opposition leader until 1955, chiefly in order to prevent Herbert Morrison, his deputy, from succeeding. This was the 'streak of cruelty' coming out again late in life, in an extraordinary and uncharacteristic display of spite. It also caused grave injury to the Labour Party, because it allowed the Bevanite splits to worsen when a new and younger leader would have moved in much earlier.

But old habits die hard in all parties, and there is nothing exclusively Labour in this vindictive urge for spite and vengeance. Iain Macleod, when he was editor of the weekly *Spectator*,* wrote a highly critical piece about Harold Macmillan's obstinacy and spitefulness in a similar situation in the Conservative Party. Macmillan, said Macleod, held on longer than he should have in order deliberately to prevent 'Rab' Butler from ever succeeding as Prime Minister. It seemed a cruel and uncharitable motive; Macmillan had previously beaten Butler to the punch when he grabbed the leadership after Eden's resignation. Even in the jungle of politics once is enough and twice a lot when it comes to killing off another's rightful claims to lead the herd. And Butler was deprived three times. As things turned out, if Macmillan had been happy to go after five years with full honours he would have avoided much of the more squalid controversy of the final two years. After five years he could have gone out with the pipes and drums celebrating great victories and reforms. Like the rest of them, he found it difficult to know when to signal: 'Mission Successfully Accomplished. Return to base.' Long-running Prime Ministers become oddly dangerous in spirit about their natural successors when they become old men: Attlee over Morrison, Macmillan over Butler, and even Churchill started raising petulant queries over Eden in order to delay having to say farewell to all his yesterdays.

In his heart of hearts Eden knew that he had paid a heavy price for Churchill's obstinate refusal to leave No. 10 Downing Street, or, earlier, to surrender the prospect, as Opposition leader, of getting back there some day. Additionally, Churchill was about the most hopeless Opposition leader in my time. This was how Eden saw the scene in his diaries: 'The vows they make earlier that they would give way to a younger man when the years begin to blunt their faculties, when illness begins to twist their judgment, these they choose to ignore. Power has become a habit they cannot bear to cast off. What neither he nor I could have foreseen

* *Spectator*, 17 January 1964.

was that when at last I stepped into his place I should have so short a run.'* There lies the clue to one of the human tragedies of power.

It was out of character that Harold Wilson, a devoted observer of the Macmillan style of leadership, did not benefit from the experience of the other's experience. But he, too, did not know when to make his excuses and leave. He had a most successful and impressive Premiership from 1964 to 1970. He had made politics exciting, he had accomplished much, not least in keeping Labour in one piece and making the party acceptable and respectable in the national mind as the 'natural party of power'. If he had decided after that to phase himself out gradually, in a state of relaxed statecraft, conditioning the party to his honourable exit, he would have provided a much more attractive figure in history: he would have avoided the more squalid and bitter controversies which saddened and distorted his final years. Quite apart from the disagreeable whispers over land speculation and reclamation, and the personal lives of his kitchen cabinet at No. 10 Downing Street, one is confident that the Wilson of 1970 would never have committed the blunders and misjudgments over the extra-ordinary Honours Lists which so disfigured his final departure. It is sad that in Wilson's case, as happened to so many other Premiers, the classic blunders at the end of the journey are remembered and the considerable achievements and sometimes glory of the early personality are forgotten.

A drug-like craving for power and the glamour of fame affects Prime Ministers of all parties. Ramsay MacDonald, three times Prime Minister, held on well beyond the moment when his growing infirmities of mind and body were only too obvious and painful. Unlike Churchill, who had a numerous entourage dedicated to concealing the full nature of *his* disabilities, MacDonald could not afford such an expensive inner guard to nurse him and cosset his whims. After his major stroke as Prime Minister, which struck while presiding over a State function at No. 10, Churchill was spirited away in secret to Chartwell, in case the photographers might have identified Lord Moran and other eminent doctors visiting No. 10. No similar back-up existed for MacDonald who, in obvious weakness, insisted on performing his duties as Prime Minister in the Commons and elsewhere where his declining powers of mind, physique and eyesight could not be concealed.

I can confirm how painful it was to see Churchill and MacDonald, piteously ill men, still struggling to appear in command when their faculties had already rotted. In Churchill's case there was the irony of time's justice: no one was more merciless in goading and gloating over MacDonald's decline than Churchill. In old age Churchill was an even more pitiful spectacle.

* *The Eden Memoirs, The Reckoning* (Cassell).

There was this distinction, however: MacDonald never intended to hold on until well beyond the point of the final crack-up. I clearly understood from him at the time—and I knew him closely from my contacts with him at Lossiemouth when I was a young reporter—that he intended to remain Premier only until the National Government had dealt with the 'economic blizzard'. Then he proposed that the parties should return to their normal pattern. But the irony was that he became indispensable to the *appearance* of the National Government, and was supported as Prime Minister until 1935, well beyond his original planned time-scale.

Among the Prime Ministers of the century Stanley Baldwin was the only one who made his resignation known for about a year before the event, which avoided any suspicion that he was being hurried off the stage against his will. He subscribed to Peel's opinion that five years should be the maximum. In his case, three times Prime Minister, he remained beyond in order to deal with the Abdication of King Edward VIII and the Coronation of King George VI, arranged the scenario for Neville Chamberlain's succession, and then departed in a blaze of glory and hallelujahs, the only one to experience such a national glow of adulation at the going down of the sun. Alas, in a couple of years, the all-party veneration was replaced by bitter recrimination, despite the fact that for two decades he had represented the mood, ambitions and ideals of a nation. His old rival, Attlee, as ever punched home the moral in a brief, seven-word headline, his style of communication: 'The John Bull Who Carried the Can.'

One final moral to be drawn from this analysis: of the seventeen Prime Ministers of this century, very few of them left No. 10 Downing Street as happy, contented and fulfilled men. The reason was all too apparent. They never knew when they were at their peak, when to make the exit in dignity, honour and even glory. By desperately holding on too long, they were overtaken by the lengthening shadows of eventide. Yet once released from the exhaustions of supreme power many of them, although they seemed to be infirm and dying when they left office, survived to enjoy glorious Indian summers: in this century Asquith, Lloyd George, Baldwin, Churchill, Eden, Attlee and Macmillan. The paradox: that they were rejuvenated by the elixir of power once they had sacrificed its symbols.

2

THE PATHOLOGY
OF POWER

Taken over the years, the health record of Prime Ministers is appalling, many times worse than that of ordinary people. Of the dozen I have known at first-hand, far too many left No. 10 Downing Street physical and nervous wrecks. Indeed, if the test is extended to all the seventeen Premiers of the twentieth century the total of those afflicted with grave illnesses is frightening. This clinical record raises sombre questions about their state of body and mind when crucial decisions affecting Britain and the world had to be taken, because all too frequently their illnesses were of a nature which must have impaired their judgments and clouded their mental clarity. Yet this inter-relationship between power, leadership and sickness is the most neglected area in histories, biographies and diaries. Far too often the details of illnesses were hushed up at the time, protected as official secrets, as the great unmentionable. In the world of commerce, on the statistics available, actuaries would insist on high-risk premiums to protect a company (in our case, the country) against the risk of seriously ill, gravely incapacitated and even dying men making important decisions. Any multinational corporation whose successive chairmen and chief executives had such alarming case-histories of major operations, nervous break-downs or other physical crack-ups would long ago have insisted on the most rigorous safeguards, including early retirement or prudent transfer to alternative employment.

 The importance of this subject to the whole world of power and statesmanship has been neglected in all the histories of our great men, and figures not at all in the studies of politics on the inside—though it has been professionally examined in medical though not in politico-power terms by two* distinguished doctors, R. Scott Stevenson and Hugh L'Etang, whose books more than ten years ago covered the health records

* (i) *Famous illnesses in History*, R. Scott Stevenson (Eyre). (ii) *The Pathology of Leadership*, Hugh L'Etang (Heinemann Medical Books).

of British, American and European leaders, including generals, admirals and air-marshals in war-time. Even the frequency and severity of the strokes suffered by Sir Winston Churchill would never have been fully known but for his doctor, Lord Moran, flouting medical tradition by publishing his famous diaries laying bare his patient's disturbing medical history over many years.* The Moran testament helps to a better understanding of Churchill the man against the back-drop of history.

CASUALTY LIST OF PMS
The casualty list besides Churchill is formidable. As has been said, Ramsay MacDonald was in total mental and physical decay during his last two years as Prime Minister, by far the most heart-rending deterioration displayed in public I have ever seen. Campbell-Bannerman, Bonar Law, MacDonald and Neville Chamberlain all died within months of resigning, two of them, Law and Chamberlain, dying from cancer which developed with alarming rapidity. Thus the determination to survive and hold on to power undoubtedly kept Sir Winston going long after the best doctors in the land pronounced him a dying man after strokes, even defying all pressures upon him to resign, whereas in the case of the four other Prime Ministers resignations were followed by death almost at once. The retention of power kept Churchill going and gave him the will to live; when it was cut off others lost the will to survive.

Baldwin lived for most of his Premiership in a constant and fluctuating state of nervous exhaustion bordering on nervous breakdowns and latterly was incapacitated by arthritis. Attlee had the bad luck of being ill in hospital at the peak of political crises; he was away for a prostate operation during the crucial period coinciding with the outbreak of war in 1939, and was again in hospital, this time with duodenal ulcers, in 1951, when two Cabinet Ministers, Aneurin Bevan and Harold Wilson and a Minister outside Cabinet, John Freeman, resigned. And then at 72 he suffered a stroke which hastened his resignation as Labour leader. Sir Anthony Eden was a wreck nervously and physically when he resigned after Suez in 1957, aggravated by earlier gall-bladder and bile duct operations which went wrong. Harold Macmillan was luckier when he went through his operation for gall-stones in 1953, though he had to resign as PM when in hospital for a prostate operation in 1963.

Of the seventeen Prime Ministers of this century only two, Sir Alec Douglas-Home and Edward Heath, left No 10 Downing Street in as good shape as when they entered. As for the other fifteen, the demands and exhaustions of power exacted a remorseless price. Lord Beaverbrook, as always, had the flair for telling the story in a single sentence: 'In the

*Winston Churchill, Lord Moran (Constable).

41

moment of supreme triumph decline begins to do its work.'* Probably Baldwin and Peel, two good judges, saw the political, personal and health problems in the right time-scale; they considered that no Prime Minister should serve in the highest office longer than five years. If this rule could be tested by hindsight the two great warrior statesmen, Lloyd George and Churchill, would have gone at the peak of their powers and avoided the squalid controversies which distorted their reputations at the end; and MacDonald, Baldwin, Macmillan and Wilson would have said their goodbyes at the height of their achievements. The secret of knowing when not to dwell upon the manner of their going has always defied the men of power. From Sir Henry Campbell-Bannerman in the early years of the century to Sir Harold Wilson seventy years later the health hazards impose a heavy price.

WILSON'S ILLNESSES

I include Sir Harold Wilson in this study of the impact of health upon the exercise, retention, and final surrender of power because of the mystery which surrounded his resignation, first announced in the most unexpected circumstances on 16 March, 1976, and then effective constitutionally on the 5 April, 1976, when James Callaghan was elected leader of the Labour Party. No convincing explanation was given at the time to explain the appearance of a rushed and surprise decision, and none has been offered since. The circumstances and personal reasons for his resignation were the more mysterious because Wilson enjoyed above all others *being* Prime Minister.

For myself, I am in no doubt that health was a major factor, although in Wilson's case, as in so many others, health was treated with utmost secrecy as a State-protected subject. I do not suggest that he resigned when he did—when all the drama of an apparently rushed and shock decision added to the excitement—because he was a sick man. But there is no doubt that health, especially his *likely future health* if he did not reduce the extraordinary pace of his activities, was a significant factor in the final decision. Its importance should not be under-rated. He could have gone on, perhaps by up to two years, but at increasing risk. In due course Lord Stone, his physician for more than twenty years, may decide to follow the example of Lord Moran, in the case of Churchill, and fill in the clinical history which could explain much about the Wilson mystery.

There is a common pattern in the series of Sir Harold's illnesses, indispositions and upsets, about half-a-dozen in all, which most medical writers interpreting such symptoms and situations for the lay mind would describe as psychosomatic in character. The first occasion when he be-

Decline and Fall of Lloyd George, Lord Beaverbrook (Collins).

came ill without any advance warning was in December 1974. He was attending a European summit conference in Paris when he complained of discomfort in the chest, a kind of persistent 'hiccup'. It was so unexpected and insistent that, unusual for him, *he* asked for Dr Stone (who always accompanied the Prime Minister on overseas visits) to be sent for. The doctor, who later described his patient to me as a 'very tough cookie in medical terms', attributed the symptoms to overstrain, overwork, inadequate rest, at the end of a year when he had fought two general elections and resumed the responsibilities of the Premiership.

So the Prime Minister was ordered to lighten the load, cut back on his speeches and journeys—before then he invariably spent most weekends stomping all over the country making major Government and party speeches to boost morale at the grassroots—and limit his TV and radio appearances. Official engagements inseparable from the job went ahead as normal. Only a few experienced observers noticed the difference, for speeches were not coming with their former regularity, timed to capture headlines in the Sunday papers and the weekend TV and radio programmes. They saw the unusual and out-of-character low profile as part of the easing off which men nudging sixty, or beyond (Wilson was then fifty-eight), exposed to high strain and tension, are advised to do.

In Harold Wilson's case, however, the warning symptoms returned spasmodically. For instance, the night before West Germany's Chancellor Schmidt was due for a weekend visit to Chequers in late 1974 Wilson felt ill again with the complaint first experienced in Paris. Its onset caused concern, so much so that serious consideration was given by him and his advisers to phoning Chancellor Schmidt, then at Hamburg preparing for the flight, asking him to postpone the Chequers meeting. But the Prime Minister quickly recovered and the Anglo-German talks went on as planned. Always hypersensitive to Press speculation, he was alive to the inevitable inquiries and rumour-mongering which would have been triggered by any last-minute cancellation of Chancellor Schmidt's visit.

To avoid any of the more observant newspapermen noticing that he was not in top form, on Sir Joseph Stone's advice he cut back drastically on his outside engagements—extra-mural and showing-the-flag speaking engagements and personal appearances—and concentrated increasingly on putting on impressive and colourful Parliamentary performances. Plans for his twice-weekly jousts with the Conservative Opposition's leader, Mrs Margaret Thatcher, during the Prime Minister's questions in the Commons on Tuesdays and Thursdays, were well prepared and discussed in advance, down to thinking up witty and mickey-taking replies to her hypothetical questions. He came to see these as his virility symbol. Sharp, gay, clever, rumbustious replies, deceptively brilliant because they

43

flew from his lips in apparent effortless spontaneity, ensured the Press stories and headlines and TV news-comments which were planned for with such accuracy. Harold in Top Form; PM's Brilliant Sallies; Wilson's Wit Rakes Maggie—the headlines wrote themselves to the reports from the Westminster front, and viewers were told most nights how he was out-shining and out-smarting the Opposition leader. The formula paid off handsomely. Never a hint leaked out about his health. He was seen as the parliamentary and political master, in form par excellence. Over nearly thirty years' experience of knowing him well and seeing him regularly at close quarters I came to identify the tell-tale signs of over-strain in his inflamed eyelid, a nervous manifestation of the old-fashioned stye. But beyond this merely superficial and transient swelling and red discolora-tion, even the best observer in the business never latched on to the real secret.

After the early chest disturbances Wilson started to joke to his closest aides about his 'hiccups', assured by his doctor that his heart was sound and strong. But the good health he had always enjoyed was obviously be-coming less invulnerable. What a layman would describe as 'nervous attacks'—stomach upsets coinciding with his self-described hiccups, for instance—affected him on several occasions. Oddly enough, they always occurred when he was on the point of attending international meetings of major importance. They never affected him, for example, before crisis meetings of the Cabinet, the Labour Party's National Execu-tive, or of the Parliamentary party, however controversial or crucial these were for his Government, and his own authority and political survival. These indeed he always enjoyed, and he never failed to savour the superb professionalism which he always produced on such occasions. Similarly, he faced the well-known physical dangers of visits to Ulster without turn-ing a hair. On the contrary, the coincidence that the upsets always took place when the more sensitive and important meetings on foreign affairs were impending—the field in which he was not first among equals—had a significance which could not be ignored.

The nature of these 'health disturbances'—I must stress they were not attacks which would have been identified by specialists as grave symp-toms requiring retirement but were seen as warning signals against over-work—had an important influence in fortifying his decision to leave office and conditioning his mind to the break. Indeed, he at first intended to announce his resignation at the Labour conference at Blackpool in the early days of October 1975. This would have equalled the excitements and theatrical drama of Harold Macmillan's resignation as Prime Minis-ter and party leader being announced at the Tory conference at Blackpool in October 1963—and he admired and envied the sense of style and impact of all the well-timed entries and exits of Mr Macmillan as the superb actor-manager with his sophisticated sense of stage-management. Constitutional advice, however, was that normally Prime Ministers do not publicly announce resignations at party assemblies or in non-Government settings; and that the Conservative precedent was only acceptable because Harold Macmillan was desperately ill in hospital for a major operation.

So Harold Wilson decided to soldier on for another few months, to cover the opening of the new session of Parliament starting a fortnight later in October 1975 and to get the new counter-inflation programme launched. But his mind was made up to go. In November and December advance dispositions were being made privately. Only Lady Wilson, Lady Falkender (Marcia Williams), his close legal friend, Lord Goodman, and Lord Stone shared the secret. In January 1976 he started making provisional forward plans in greater detail for his future life as an ex-Prime Minister. Talks took place, for instance, at No. 10 Downing Street in January on the details of his television series of programmes on former Prime Ministers when he met David Frost and TV executives, though he did not tell them of when he would go. The personal fee for this was reported to be enormous—which helped to reassure the anxieties which senior citizens and others coming up to their pensions sometimes feel about the financial hardships in maintaining standards and providing for their families.

Why such illnesses and attacks should be treated as official secrets—as happens under almost all Prime Ministers—can only be explained by the mystique of power. In Harold Wilson's case it was obvious he was getting out of condition in his late fifties. He had not played a full round of golf for three to four years, and when it was clear he had a weight problem, coinciding with his worrying chest 'hiccups', he slimmed back drastically by cutting down on his intake of food and spirits. The paradox was that when he finally left office he was actually fitter than he had been at any time for the preceding two years, but the final strain of office had been lightened by virtue of his actual decision to go, in which he was encouraged by Lady Wilson who wanted him to avoid fighting another election at all costs. And the 'hiccups' which nervously affected the heart-lungs eased off as the tensions and crises of office lessened with the prospect of freedom from care. Like his predecessors—Clem Attlee, Anthony Eden and Harold Macmillan, who all enjoyed long Indian summers after surrendering power at the top—Harold Wilson recovered new vigour and buoyancy on his escape from the exhaustions of Premiership. He showed a more placid and relaxed acceptance of the inevitability of resignation than most of his predecessors at No. 10.

No one fought more desperately to hold on to office than Sir Winston Churchill, long beyond the point of being a semi-invalid. As we now know, with all the medical detail filled in by Lord Moran, the Prime Minister collapsed towards the close of a dinner given at No 10 Downing Street, on Wednesday, 23 June, 1953, in honour of Signor de Gasperi, Prime Minister of Italy. After making a perfect and gay little speech, full of wit and banter, without notes, he slumped in his chair; one side of his mouth drooped but, though unable to rise to his feet, he was able to go through all the gestures of saying goodbye to the chief guests individually, with that kindness and respect characteristic of him. A stroke was diagnosed—Winston was then 78—but there were high hopes that he would speedily recover, as he had from an earlier seizure in 1948. Over the following two days, after being moved to Chartwell, he became steadily worse, and the paralysis became more widespread. Indeed, his condition became so grave that on Friday, 25 June, 1953, Moran warned the Churchill family and his personal staff, headed by Sir John Colville, Principal Private Secretary, that Winston could not be expected to survive the weekend. That was the very day that Sir Anthony Eden, the Crown Prince, was going through his major operation in Boston, which kept him off duty until the autumn.

The country thus faced the unprecedented position of having simultaneously a Prime Minister apparently dying, with his successor-designate seriously ill, certain to be an invalid for several months. To avoid a crisis atmosphere of speculation and uncertainty, leading Ministers and their top advisers became blue-pencil sub-editors in order to censor the news. This is how Lord Moran and and another famous leader of the medical profession, Sir Russell Brain, jointly drafted their medical bulletin that critical weekend:

> For a long time the Prime Minister has had no respite from his arduous duties and a disturbance of the cerebral circulation has developed, resulting in attacks of giddiness. We have therefore advised him to abandon his journey to Bermuda and to take at least a month's rest.

This was how 'Rab' (later Lord) Butler and Lord Salisbury 'doctored' the distinguished doctors' prose in order to conceal any possible clue that a stroke had occurred:

> The Prime Minister has had no respite from his arduous duties and is in need of a complete rest. We have therefore advised him to abandon his journey to Bermuda and to lighten his duties for at least a month.

At the same time emergency plans went ahead in secret, masterminded by Sir John Colville, for Lord Salisbury to take over as a 'pro tem' Prime

Minister until such time as Anthony Eden should recover and take up the succession. This programme for an interim Premier was designed to prevent 'Rab' Butler establishing himself at No 10 in case he liked the job so much that he might be disinclined to move out for 'dear Anthony'.

Lord Moran required a massive book of over 800 pages to give all the details as Churchill's doctor. It is a disturbing history, for it reveals how Churchill, the second most powerful man in the Western World, was for long periods a sick, ailing and infirm man during the twenty-five years Moran was his doctor. At all times the utmost care was taken to hush up the facts. With hindsight, this is how the famous physician resolved his ethical dilemma. 'It was not until some years later that I came to see that it is not possible to follow the last twenty-five years of Wintston's life without a knowledge of his medical background. It was exhaustion of mind and body that accounts for much that is otherwise inexplicable in the last years of the war. . . . It is certain that the onset of old age and the succession of strokes explain in part why he was not more effective' as Opposition leader and later as Prime Minister.*

Sir John Colville vigorously rejects Moran's version that Churchill was often a sick man even in war-time, because as private secreary he saw much more of the great man in action than did Moran. Even so, the medical case-book presented by the famous doctor must cause widespread fears that truth is always the first casualty when it comes to concealing the real state of health of our Prime Ministers. The Moran diaries revealed the full clinical record of Churchill's seizures, strokes and major illnesses which would have otherwise remained a Downing Street secret.

Churchill's medical history became even more bizarre when Moran recounted the angry reactions in Downing Street when the newspapers finally latched on to the fact that the Prime Minister was severely incapacitated. The *Daily Mirror* in particular roused Churchill's ire when it publicised American reports about the strokes and demanded: 'Is there any reason why the British people should not be told the facts about the health of their Prime Minister? . . . Let us know whether Sir Winston Churchill is fit enough to lead us.' Yet Churchill still resisted all pressures and advice that he should retire: 'Twilight of a Giant' as the *Mirror* headlined the plight, a 'Giant in Decay' 'A Dying Gladiator'. It was only when Cabinet colleagues and party chiefs put him under irresistible pressure that he decided to retire—and even then he complained to Moran that Eden was pushing him out!

The proposal was seriously canvassed at one time that to save him from the constant strain of political battles in the Commons Churchill might go to the Lords—I recall that at the time the newspapers speculated whether

* *Churchill, The Struggle for Survival*, Lord Moran (Constable).

a Dukedom would be the most appropriate—and allow Eden to be in command in the lower chamber and run himself in for the top job later. The project was rapidly discarded. Having a Prime Minister in the Lords in the modern age would have been regarded as unacceptable. But the suggestion had a long honourable lineage, because it was also seriously recommended fifty years earlier, by King Edward VII, for another seriously ailing Prime Minister, Sir Henry Campbell-Bannerman, leader of the great Liberal Government of 1905. In the earlier case, too, the news of the grave illness was kept secret, despite the Prime Minister's record of heart attacks, high blood pressure, and frequent bouts of asthma. He was the Prime Minister who came nearest to dying in office; he resigned on 6 April, 1908 (after two years of constant illness), and died on 22 April. The situation was captured by his official biographer, J. A. Spender, the famous Liberal journalist: 'The Government of the country was carried on with the sick Prime Minister unable to see or consult with his colleagues. Cabinets were summoned without reference to him and decisions taken with such consultation by deputy or in writing, as circumstances permitted, and often none was possible.'*

RESIGNATIONS AND FATAL MALADIES

Two Prime Ministers, Bonar Law in 1923 and Neville Chamberlain in 1940, died almost immediately after resigning. Indeed, the cases of four Prime Ministers, Campbell-Bannerman, Law, Chamberlain and Mac-Donald, raise the important question about the degree to which our national leaders became predisposed to suffer grave and often fatal illnesses after experiencing not only the loss of office but also the personal agony of bereavement and emotional and physical exhaustion. The contemporary records tell how Campbell-Bannerman severely overtaxed himself by personally nursing his wife through her fatal illness and afterwards was inconsolable. Bonar Law remained a broken man too, a weary, depressed figure, after losing his wife, and then his two sons on active service. The end came with devasting swiftness. He became Prime Minister on 23 October, 1922. Early in the new year throat cancer was diagnosed. He resigned on 22 May 1923 and died on 30 October 1923.

Chamberlain died only months after being cruelly and humiliatingly rejected by Parliament and his party from a disease which gave no advance warning when he was Prime Minister; certainly there was no evidence to show how long his strength had been sapped by cancer, and the extent to which his character and judgment had been impaired in consequence during the pressure and failure of his appeasement policies. Iain Macleod, in his biography of Chamberlain, recounts how his 'political

* *Campbell-Bannerman*, J. A. Spender (Hodder and Stoughton).

48

overthrow and all it meant in terms of distress proved mortal'.* He fell from power on 10 May, 1940; on 10 June his diary records for the first time 'considerable pain in the abdomen'; on 24 July X-rays revealed a partial stricture of the bowel and an exploratory operation was ordered. On 9 September he returned to No 11 a partially crippled man knowing that the cancerous growth which had caused the trouble was inoperable and incurable. He resigned from public life on 3 October. The end came sooner than he had been told. He died on 9 November.

Iain Macleod added: 'Years later, another famous doctor was to write this: "I have slowly come to frame in my mind an aphorism that can never be stated as such, because no statistics can be advanced to support it: 'The happy man never gets cancer. The instances where the first recognisable onset of cancer has followed almost immediately on some disaster, a bereavement, the break-up of a relationship, a financial crisis, or an accident, are so numerous that they suggest that some controlling force that has hitherto kept the outbreak . . . in check has been removed.'

After quoting the experience and judgments of Sir Heneage Ogilvie, in his Ward Jones lecture, 'The Human Heritage', at Manchester University in 1957, Iain Macleod added: 'Cause and effect cannot be proved, but in Neville Chamberlain's case the suddenness of physical collapse in a constitution hitherto so tough and wiry could certainly be taken as *prima facie* evidence of the truth of Sir Heneage Ogilvie's aphorism.' During the many appeasement crises he suffered painful attacks constantly from gout and neuralgia.

Ramsay MacDonald also died only months after leaving office, killed by a stroke while on a cruise to South America in search of health. Many Premiers seem to lose the will to live when compelled to leave office, losing status, authority and acclaim in what they consider cruel circumstances. Because of the exhaustions of his pioneering leadership struggles when forming the Labour Party from a collection of warring groups and cliques, followed by the persecution of his peace stand in the First World War, then the strains of his two minority Governments leading to the agonies suffered when he broke with his own party on forming the National Government in 1931, MacDonald went into rapid mental and physical deterioration, the more astonishing in one who had previously showed such stamina and strength. It was a most distressing collapse, the penalty for a lifetime's overwork and overstrain. In the final stages of his Premiership he often lost the thread of his speeches as his memory would flag or snap. Even four years before the final collapse his memory was failing; in 1931 he forgot the name of the Canadian Prime Minister who was staying with him at Chequers for the weekend. This upset him ter-

* *Neville Chamberlain*, Iain Macleod (Muller).

ribly: 'My brain is going.' When he lost the thread of a speech he would turn to Baldwin sitting beside him on the Front Bench and ask what the MPs were laughing at, mocked and barracked by his old Labour comrades and not defended by his new Conservative and Liberal allies. His glaucoma, for which he went through an operation in 1931, required officials to read documents to him. It was so bad in 1935 and 1936 that he had to hold official statements and replies a couple of inches from his eyes, while his critics jeered in merriment at his discomfiture as though the sad break-up of one who had exerted a decisive influence in shaping the twentieth century were a huge but sick political joke. He was frequently at the point of collapse. Because of the glaucoma he was banned from reading Government documents for months at a time. Baldwin walked into his room one day in the Commons and found him lying asleep on a couch with papers spread around. Baldwin insisted that the staff should observe complete secrecy about this and similar incidents. 'The Prime Minister,' wrote Hankey, the Cabinet secretary, 'has been very seedy, and when under nervous strain he is apt to vomit in the mornings and this leaves him terribly weak.'*

I have never seen a Prime Minister suffer more than MacDonald from MPs' cruelty and total lack of Christian charity and understanding. Baldwin's biographers described the MPs as 'like crabs (which) turn to eat the sick and wounded among them'. It was my first experience of how crude politicians can become in their unfeeling hatreds; it was a frightening initiation for a young journalist into the agonies that public life brings to all too many. Politics has no place in its primitive ritual for the grace of sympathy.

NERVOUS EXHAUSTION

Even Stanley Baldwin, behind the relaxed style of a phlegmatic countryman, scratching pigs' backs to keep them happy, was unbelievably tense, which explained the constant twitching of the nose, facial distortions, the loud snapping of the fingers, nervous grimaces, and the profuse sweating which always occurred before big set orations. His son wrote, commenting upon some journalist's comments about his father's 'bovine passivity which nothing could ever disturb', had this to say: 'If they could have seen him closely when he was summoning up his reserves to face an ordeal too great for his thinly spread forces . . . they would have marvelled that a man could hold such a strain. Before an important speech the colour would leave his face, the sweat would sometimes roll off his brow, and he has confessed that time and again he felt he might be sick.'* On occasion he had to use all his powers to prevent himself rushing from the scene

* *Baldwin*, Keith Middlemas & John Barnes (Weidenfeld).

'from sheer panic nerves'.* He lived for much of his Premiership on the edge of nervous breakdowns; indeed, he returned from a three-month convalescence to recover his nervous balance in time to cope with the Abdication crisis, which he handled with the most relaxed appearance of self-assurance. The diaries of the period reveal many scares about the state of his health and imminent collapses. He learned to pace himself better than most Prime Ministers, thus preserving his scant resources for the major trials. The *Dictionary of National Biography* summed up his formula like this: 'His lethargy was often a mask to cover impulsive, emotional and exhausting spurts of nervous energy . . . incapable of prolonged continuous effort.' Yet he remained the classic interpreter of England and the common man, thanks to regular and long holidays to recharge the flat nerve batteries and thus avoid the total nervous breakdowns forever feared by his doctors. When he finally retired in 1937 he took a long time to recover from nervous exhaustion.

EDEN'S HEALTH RECORD
Sir Anthony Eden was plagued by bad health, concealed behind the debonair style of permanent youth, for most of his public life, and his physical and nervous resources were in no state to enable him to withstand the final humiliations. Eden indeed is the most notable case where the question may seriously be posed whether he was not already, at the time he became Premier, so over-stretched and overwrought, a sick man in mind and body, as to make it impossible for him to be in command of himself, or events. Long before he succeeded Sir Winston Churchill he had had a series of weakening high fevers, illnesses and operations. These must have sapped his slim resources which made the final smash-up inevitable during his brief run as Prime Minister. In the later stages of his career he was all too obviously a broken man, living on his nerves and constantly on the point of breakdown, a complete contrast with the buoyant Eden I knew and reported before the war. His was the most tragic health story of all. Not a year passed from 1944 onwards without his being laid low by a wide variety of illnesses—fevers, jaundice, influenza, operations—yet he continued the struggle for survival with undiminished courage. Even at the peak of Suez in 1956 he had to spend the crucial make-or-break weekend in hospital with an ominous 105 degrees temperature—and then insisted on returning to No. 10 before he was fit. And only a couple of months after the Suez disaster he was forced into resignation by a total health breakdown. He paid the price for neglecting his health, forever driving himself beyond the point of endurance. Even the gall bladder operation which led to his inevitable collapse might have been better con-

* *My Father*, A. W. Baldwin (Allen & Unwin).

51

trolled if he had sought attention earlier; the delay allowed the stone to move from the gall bladder into the duct, which triggered off more and more complications. As Harold Macmillan said to me twenty years later, in 1977, looking back at his predecessor: 'Anthony neglected and ruined his health in the service of his country by always postponing treatment until beyond the last minute.' His bad health had a much longer history than people imagine. Long before the war I remember there were anxieties about his stamina. I reported at the time that after a non-stop tour of Moscow, Berlin, Warsaw and Prague, he suffered from heart-strain and exhaustion, unable to report to the Cabinet for a few days, and after that he was ordered by his doctors to rest. He was then still in his thirties, when doctors do not normally look for strained hearts and nervous breakdowns in their patients. The final crack-up, climaxed by Suez, had a life-long history. At the end of the journey Eden himself gave the clue: 'Thirty years of political work at high tension and a feckless disregard for my own health were to claim their forfeit.'*

Harold Macmillan also went through a gall-stones operation, at about the same time as Eden's first one, but in his case it was completely successful; and ten years later he suffered the critical prostate operation which precipitated his resignation as Prime Minister and party leader. The prostate condition had been identified a year earlier. He was, like Baldwin, a very highly strung nervous person behind the languid Edwardian style. Before crucial debates, questions and the big-time speeches in mass settings he, too, was often overcome by sickness and nerves, the occupational hazard of those Prime Ministers with finely strung personalities; no matter how long their experience and mastery of Parliament they were susceptible to attacks of nerves, fears, and a sense of ordeal anew, sometimes accompanied by attacks of physical sickness.

KILLING PRESSURES

Even the little indiarubber man himself, Clem Attlee, had his spells of serious illness which coincidently occurred during major national and party crises, though in his case there could never be any question of cause and effect or psychosomatic tensions as affected Harold Wilson. He had a prostate operation which removed him from Parliament during the crisis-torn weeks in August and September 1939 He. was again seriously ill in 1951, undergoing duodenal ulcer surgery, when he had to cope from his hospital bed with the resignation from his Government of Aneurin Bevan, Harold Wilson and John Freeman; and at seventy-two he suffered a stroke which finally convinced him that the time had come for him to resign Labour's leadership. The Attlee case-book is relevant for another reason in the

* *The Eden Memoirs, The Reckoning* (Cassell).

inter-relation of the killing pressures between power and health. When he formed the Labour Government in 1945 he and his senior Ministers had already served for five years in Churchill's war-time Government. They paid grievously for the physical exhaustions and nervous tensions which in the end added up to ten years at the centre of power. Ernest Bevin, Foreign Secretary, suffered heart attacks and black-outs for years, often at crucial meetings and while making speeches at home and abroad, but kept going on whisky, before dying of angina pectoris. Sir Stafford Cripps, Chancellor of the Exchequer, died of spinal turberculosis after suffering from exhaustion and severe insomnia for a long time. Herbert Morrison, Home Secretary and Leader of the Commons, was laid low with leg thrombosis and lung troubles. Other Ministers also had health problems: Hugh Dalton, also Chancellor, confessed in his diaries that he was often exhausted and only kept going by hefty doses of benzedrene.

This example of how a Government was weakened and then finally destroyed by serious illnesses wiping out an entire top generation measures the time-scale between supreme power and final physical disintegration. From personal observation I should say that the nervous system is the first to crack. I also noticed from observing the Prime Ministers in close-up, that in many cases their intake of whisky and brandy is noticeably higher on leaving office than when they first entered No. 10.

James Callaghan, though older than Wilson, is staying the pace better, and keeps himself in better shape: he cut out even his minimal alcohol some years ago, and spends most weekends walking energetically around his farm. He is also more disciplined in delegating, and avoids wasting his energies chasing Ministers and interfering with Departments. I remember Richard Crossman saying to me some years ago, before Callaghan succeeded Wilson: 'Poor post-prostate Jim has had it now; he'll never make it after this. He's beyond the point of no return.' It was 'Big Jim' who made it; it was Dick Crossman who fell.

During his brief Premiership Sir Alec Douglas-Home had an excellent health record. He kept in top form by a rigorous programme of self-discipline, with plenty of exercise every weekend on his Scottish estates, and by observing almost spartan moderation in food and drink. He had better reason than most to recognise the importance of husbanding health; oddly enough, he acquired his astonishing stamina through having to lie on his back for two years with spinal tuberculosis—the best example, he liked to claim, of how surgeons could put backbone into a future Prime Minister. Lloyd George, like Macmillan, Callaghan and Attlee, was also a prostate victim, but after he had left office. But in his case the operation had a profound effect upon history, because it left him incapacitated for a long period in 1931 when the National Government was being formed by MacDonald and Baldwin. If only he had been in full vigour during the crucial months the realignment would have gone Left and not Right-of-Centre, in which eventuality the history of the thirties would have followed another destiny. Earlier in his career he suffered the agony of frequent attacks of neuralgia. Even in 1912 he wrote: 'I have had a temporary breakdown . . . much to my disappointment it is only temporary.'

Finally, Edward Heath merits only a single sentence mention in this study of the pathology of power, and is the odd man out: he was the fittest of all the Prime Ministers of the century and never had a day's illness worth mentioning throughout his ten years at the top, as Conservative leader and as Prime Minister. He really enjoyed splendid health, helped by his devotion to keeping fit by robust marine exercise and the spiritual uplift brought by great music.

3

FAREWELL TO IMPERIAL GLORY

It is difficult to measure the relative greatness and the successes and failures of the Prime Ministers discussed in the preceding chapters without seeing them, as I did, in both their domestic and global settings as Britain retreated from the might and grandeur of Empire into its rapid decline. Today scarcely a vestige remains to remind our children and grandchildren of a small offshore island's splendour in a saga of Imperial greatness. Yet in one brief life-time it had happily shed its history as a world power and opted peacefully, almost with relief, for a secondary status. This is not bitter-sweet nostalgia for all our yesterdays. It is history.

First, take the giants, Lloyd George and Winston Churchill. They were world statesmen in their own right, massive figures in history, not only because they led their country and the free world to victory in two world wars but also because they were the leaders—separated by a quarter of a century—of the greatest Imperial power ever seen on this earth. Lloyd George was the co-equal of President Wilson of the United States and 'Tiger' Clemenceau, the saviour of France, during and immediately after the First World War; Churchill was one of the 'Big Three' with Franklin D. Roosevelt and Stalin in the Second. They were the outstanding warrior-statesmen of world history. So in trying to strike a balance between them and our peace-time Premiers we must recognise that Ramsay MacDonald, Stanley Baldwin and Neville Chamberlain were projected on the world stage because of the Imperial might they represented. By comparison, latter-day leaders such as Harold Wilson, Edward Heath and James Callaghan must be seen in an entirely different power game as the result of Britain slipping from the prestige of world class to the drab and dreary struggle for survival well down the hierarchy of nations. So the world frontiers have gone, the global horizons have disappeared. The magnitude of this retreat from greatness is still too close to be assessed by the new generations. It has all happened at staggering speed, with each day's new history unfolding before one's eyes, with compelling urgency, and recorded for next morning's newspapers.

Those days are recalled as a contribution by an old reporter to a better understanding of what it was like when great history was being made. As Lord Beaverbrook wrote in his *Men and Power*: 'It may be asked: "Were you there?" I was there.' Having known all the principal figures at first-hand I reported them and the events of their time while the impressions were clear, and instant, not as rationalised by hindsight. Winston Churchill once ruefully commented: 'We are a people of short memories.' Already the story of Britain's mighty imperial power is being forgotten; schools and colleges nowadays pay scant attention to British achievements of the past over five continents and seven seas. Could this be a hand-up from the so-called 'guilt complex' about Colonialism? We salute the 'glory that was Greece, the grandeur that was Rome' and the faculties at our high centres of learning pay much attention to other Empires, whether Roman, Nordic, Iberian, Mediterranean, Napoleonic, and so on; but whether from embarrassment or escapism the achievements of the British Empire are rarely recalled.

FULFILLED DESTINY

Several impressive books have been written about the eclipse of the British Empire as it took place and affected the great centres of Empire— India, Africa and elsewhere—notably James Morris's trilogy, finalised in *Farewell the Trumpets—An Imperial Retreat*. These have been chiefly concerned with events as they unfolded in the outposts of the British Raj and in the powerful Colonial capitals. But at the heart of Empire, in the Mother of Parliaments at Westminster, the transformation from Imperial glory to the inward-looking assembly of today was conducted with astonishing lack of emotion, passion, anger or regret, and least of all nostalgia, over Britain's might before decline and fall set in, but in a relaxed realistic mood under both Tory and Labour Governments, as they fulfilled Britain's destiny by lowering the Union Jack and sounding the Last Post. As a newsman at Westminister I reported and wrote about at length each chapter in the story, as thirty-six separate independence statutes were passed creating thirty-six independent peoples and countries. And the vast edifice was dismantled peacefully, without Britain—unlike earlier Empires—ever being defeated in war. The whole process was completed in barely one brief life-time, with eighty per cent concentrated into fifteen years. An astonishing achievement.

It is difficult for the new generations, the sons and daughters of those who went through the experience, to understand the vastness of the transformation—all achieved without revolution, social convulsions or political upheaval, but in a mood of resignation that the time had come to call it a day and go home. Yet in the author's professional life he has witnessed and reported greater human, national, economic and social changes than occurred over many centuries earlier.

The Parliament I left the other day is a much more inbred, confused, inward-looking and self-centred place than when I first appeared on the scene on what seems to be only the day before yesterday, when we headed the world league. Two experiences illustrate the change in character and status of Westminster. In the thirties the Diplomatic Gallery in the House of Commons was crowded twice a week, by a score of Ambassadors eager to listen to and interpret for Washington, Paris, Moscow, Berlin, Rome and other major capitals what the Prime Ministers of the period— MacDonald, Baldwin and Chamberlain—had to say on the unending series of world crises; and not to take notes only of what the Premiers and the Foreign Secretaries were saying. There were in addition giants of international standing among the backbenchers. Lloyd George and Churchill overshadowed even the front benches, but other notable figures of world renown: Leopold Amery, Sir Austen Chamberlain, Sir Robert Horne, former Premiers, party leaders, and those in the top rungs of earlier Cabinets, big figures with established reputations over the globe; the Opposition figures, like Clement Attlee and Arthur Greenwood for Labour and Clement Davies, Sir Herbert Samuel and Sir Archibald Sinclair for the Liberals, had a stature of their own.

In recent years it was fashionable to say, in economic terms, that when America sneezed the rest of the world caught pneumonia. In the inter-war period it was true to say that what Westminster said made the rest of the world sit up and take notice. This was shown by another feature of the Westminster scene then. The Parliamentary Press Gallery, the Members' Lobby and corridors were packed with the world newspapermen, not because they liked our beer but because Westminster was the biggest source of news and power in the world. (This subject is more fully studied in Chapter on The Lobby.) Now that the lengthening shadows have overtaken our Imperial mission and world role those two great sensitive barometers, the Ambassadors and the world newsmen who crowded Westminster, measuring world crises and national power have paid their respects and moved on. For many years few Ambassadors have been seen around the Palace of Westminister, apart from new envoys appointed to the Court of St James's who look in out of curiosity and to satisfy the interest of their wives and children in quaint old buildings and customs of the olde worlde. I doubt whether many could find their way to Westminster or discover the stairs to their own Westminster Gallery. Similar experience applies to the world newspapermen. They find little at

Westminster today likely to interest their people back home apart from the occasional piece about the United Kingdom's domestic economic and union problems; they have moved on to the new countries of Africa and Asia and the power centres of Europe at Brussels and Strasbourg, Bonn and Paris.

But until the Imperial retreat world affairs dominated Westminster, which was geared to Empire and the world to an extent impossible for the present generation to imagine. Until the post-war era the most prestigious members of all Cabinets of all parties were the Secretary of State for India, the Secretary of State for the Dominions, the Secretary of State for the Colonies. The Secretaries for *what*? The quaint old titles puzzle today's readers. But in the days of world dominion these Ministers headed the pecking order; the most influential members of the Cabinet promoted from the more colourless Departments of State on the home front. The writ of each ruled continents and oceans. The world frontiers they represented dominated the attention of Parliament and of the Press; every year the big showpieces at the Conservative Party conferences were the wide-ranging debates on India, Dominions and Colonies, appropriate for a party which identified itself as the true-blue party of Empire and Britain's Imperial mission. Oddly, there were no colour or racist complexes around in those days. The most important events in the British calendar were the regular conferences of the Dominion and Commonwealth Prime Ministers, the prelude to modern Summitry on the grand scale. Then the Prime Ministers of the UK would never dream of taking major decisions of world significance without first consulting the Premiers of Canada, Australia, New Zealand and South Africa. According to the Cabinet records now available, this process took place almost weekly, and often announcements drafted for the Westminster Parliament were delayed until the reactions and comments came back from the 'White' Commonwealth—and then duly amended.

In the brief perspective of history covered by this journalist in Parliament and Whitehall, scarcely a vestige of the old massive Imperial structure remains to remind our young people of the vast sweep of British history. Yet overseas there are 990 million people who owe their independence, Government, culture, maturity and all the services of a modern State to Britain and the Westminster model. Historians will no doubt find it difficult to explain that the vast de-Colonialisation was completed without any of the modern bitterness and hatred over colour and race. I never heard the prejudices aroused by these emotive words until the 1960s and 1970s. By then the history of the Empire was all neatly filed away in the archives, of interest only to research students. There were, of course, a few conflicts like that of Mau-Mau in Kenya and elsewhere, but in the broad sweep of history the run-down of Imperial glory was achieved constitutionally and with goodwill.

The most remarkable feature of this vast world-wide liquidation of an Empire was that Westminster never followed a masterplan, for none ever existed. One feels that inadequate attention has yet been paid to the imaginative genius and vision which produced final independence. Here is a typical British paradox. The transformation was inspired not by wild freedom fighters and tribal rebellion and revolution, but by the old governing families who might have been expected to respond to atavistic voices and use force if need be to preserve old Imperial majesty. The process started in the middle of the last century by the Earl of Durham's historic report on Canada, which set out in detail the idealistic framework for self-governing Dominions and the White Commonwealth which followed. Following the Durham reforms, Lord Balfour in the 1920s produced the plan for self-governing Dominions and the independence of the Colonies. Their historical dream was not to face-lift the old Empire under a new name but to form an association of free peoples and independent nations to form a Commonwealth because they had the shared experience of once having been ruled by the British Mother of Parliaments and were heirs to the British traditions of freedom.

INDIA REFORM BILL
This background explains why one of my first full Parliamentary sessions in the early 1930s was devoted almost exclusively to covering the passing of the India Reform Bill, which laid the foundations of the total independence of the sub-continent fifteen years later. The sequence is revealing. The lesson from that opening exercise which set the pattern for finally sequestrating the Empire, which I first reported as a youngster, has a sharp relevance to life at Westminster today. For many months on end, every day, every night and all night, between seventy and eighty Right-wing Tory MPs opposed every word, clause and page of the formidable Bill—it was the largest of all time with 386 pages, 451 clauses, and endless schedules—the biggest and most persistent rebellion on record. The point of importance for today's Commons is that this mass insurrection and defiance on India did not result in expulsions, withdrawal of Whips, or drumhead trials for MPs repudiated by constituency associations for desertion in action. When the Bill was finally passed the rebels accepted the verdict of history and regrouped as loyal members of their party. (There was one notable exception to this reconciliation, Sir Winston Churchill, whose role in the history of the thirties is studied in detail in Chapter 8.)

Is it conceivable in modern political conditions at Westminster for such a massive revolt to take place over such a long time without destroying party unity, leading to witch-hunts, splits, and discipline trials as well as other sacrifices to the political gods? The moral comes through the years: it is that at the centre there was much greater freedom and independence allowed to individual party MPs than is conceivable today. As the power of the Executive, Whips, and party machines has increased remorselessly the remnants of individual independence have been finally wiped out. The much tougher independence which was then possible and tolerable before the strong-arm centralised machines moved in was encouraged by the presence of some twelve Independent members from the Universities, major personalities in their own right with established reputations in public life. The abolition of the University franchise, in 1948, was a major loss to the spirit and status of independence which spilled off on other parties. It is impossible today to imagine successors of Harold Macmillan, to cite one example of the thirties, resigning the Whip in protest against his Government's policies, attacking and deriding his Ministers for years, and then rejoining the ranks when the party had caught up with him and not him with the party—and ending up as a long-running Prime Minister!

PARLIAMENT THEN AND NOW
More evidence to show the transformation which has taken place from the Imperial Parliament at its zenith to the very narrow spectrum of today's is to compare the daily Westminster programme of then and now. The daily question hour, regarded as the show-piece of democracy, tells the story of how world, Imperial and Colonial affairs dominated the Westminster scene and occupied MPs' minds. Let *Hansard* itself tell the story. The following extract for a week in July 1935 was picked at random:

Monday, 8th July: The question session opened with India, Aden, Abyssinia and Mussolini; Russia, Austria, British Somaliland, Argentine Railway loans, Western Europe air pact, League of Nations, Tanganyika. These were balanced with home front questions on agriculture, milk marketing board's finances, sugar beet factories, Regents Park amenities. Scottish questions, including the need to reform the Gretna Green system for runaway weddings; unemployment, mercantile marine, cotton spinning.

Tuesday, 9th: South African Protectorates, Southern Rhodesia, Labrador developments, German exports, aircraft exports, Congo basin, Abyssinia, Palestine, illegal Jewish immigrants to the Middle East; and on the home front: agriculture, motor-car insurance, Scotland's economic problems, coal crises, farm marketing schemes, education, unemployment.

Wednesday, 10th: League of Nations, naval talks, Italy and Abyssinia, air arms, Northern Rhodesia, India, Malaya, Territorial Army, Colonial investment. At home: transport, road repairs, railways, trade and commerce.

Thursday, 11th: League of Nations, the covenant, peace talks, international currencies, Palestine, Bolivia and Paraguay, Russian trade, German refugees, Mexico, Eritrea, Smyrna, China, Kenya, Cyprus, Palestine (almost daily), Seychelles. At home: trade boards, unemployment, Navy, betting and lotteries, housing, health, cotton, schools.

The same days of July, but forty-three years later, tell how world horizons have gone forever. Over the same period there was not a single question asked about anything beyond these shores, with but one notable exception to do with the European involvement: there were a couple of queries about the impact of Common Market policies on the UK fishing ports. Instead of the daily ration of questions then about Africa, Asia, the West Indies and relations with the White Commonwealth countries of Canada, Australia, New Zealand and South Africa, this is the representative daily diet for the modern generation of MPs in the very late seventies nudging into the eighties: industrial developments, relations between Trade and Industry Departments with private industries, the Post Office, the National Enterprise Board, social services. But the extent to which members have become welfare officers may be measured by this catalogue of the more personal worries which are of major concern for constituents in particular: out-patient facilities, one-parent families, disabled needs, hospital waiting lists, speech therapists, pre-school playgroups, pay beds, homocopathic provisions, funeral costs, drugs charges, merit awards for consultants, occupational deafness, planning prisons, crime, dentists, attendance allowance, meals-on-wheels, public footpaths, comprehensives, fares.

It may well be argued that MPs today are contributing more to the sum of their constituents' happiness and comfort by devoting themselves with so much energy and ardour to the endless succession of welfare and human and family problems on their doorsteps. It all depends on how one measures the scale of progress. The author remembers clearly when he was studying the humanities as a teenage reporter learning his business on the *Elgin Courant and Courier* in his home-town. It was a routine task to attend the regular meetings of the Parish Councils in the little towns and villages in the country and coastal areas of

Moray. The primary task of those Parish Councils was to relieve the personal and family cares, hardships and worries of men and women they knew at first-hand. The local councillors handled their people's problems with justice, generosity, and understanding. The Parish Councils were the first casualty of the obsession of bureaucracy over the years to reorganise and streamline local government. One of the consequences has been to provide an elevated status to the exercise. For a substantial proportion of the problems which are aired by modern MPs in the Commons chamber, and much more frequently in personal cases explained in letters to Ministers and Departmental officials, are broadly identical with those which used to be resolved in the old Parish Council office across the table.

The process produces its own paradox. As the Empire was decentralised, from being ruled from Westminster and Whitehall to local independence, the reverse pattern was being strenuously followed in the United Kingdom, with more and more power transferred not only from the old Parish Councils—for these had the stigma of Poor Law relief—but from the towns and counties which used to run their own affairs in daily contact with their communities to the new Whitehall dynasties. The vacuum created in Whitehall when we stopped running the biggest Empire on record was at once filled by the domestic show at home.

PRICE OF VICTORY

History tells how the cost of victory in two world wars accelerated the bankruptcy of Britain as a world power and the final eclipse of Empire. It was obvious to most experienced journalists that the Second World War left Britain exhausted, demoralised and confused, with all the old zest, pride and ambition for world power and Imperial glory gone forever. Almost with a sense of relief the demolition squads among Whitehall's draftsmen were called in to give the Colonial peoples their freedom.

Could the process of disintegration have been avoided? I doubt it very much. Long before Hitler and Mussolini appeared on the scene, the rot, in Imperial terms, had set in. Some years before Hitler was ever mentioned in the British papers the sun had started setting on the British Raj. Indeed, when Stanley Baldwin announced his determination to push through the first massive reforms for India I was reporting from Westminster at the same time the prophecies by all parties and personalities, including Winston Churchill and Lloyd George, that Europe faced the prospects of a generation and more of peace, as Britain, France and the United States solemnly debated how to remedy the injustices of the Versailles Treaty in order to encourage German democracy; all policies were concerned with disarmament, not rearmament.

That was the mood at Westminster when I arrived, and the policy of dismantling and modernising the Empire had started. That was the beginning of the end, not only of direct British rule over much of the world but of an outward-looking British Parliament at Westminster as well. The Second World War foreshortened the time-scale of dissolution and showed that Britain had no longer either the will or the strength to rule; to be accelerated by the 'wind of change' in Africa where the days of flying from the Cape to Cairo over an unbroken chain of countries and peoples flying the Union Jack were gone forever.

Various officials of rank in Whitehall individually claimed credit for drafting Harold Macmillan's 'wind of change' picture-phrase. They need not have bothered about their skills in ghost-writing. A few older hands at Westminster with good memories, and one newsman in particular, could recognise the distinguished pedigree in the imagery. Baldwin, in 1935, justified his determination to force through the first major reforms for India in these words: 'There is a wind of nationalism and freedom blowing round the world and blowing as strongly in Asia as anywhere in the world.' Macmillan's phrase at Cape Town in February 1960, used the words: 'The wind of change is blowing through the Continent. Whether we like it or not, the growth of naturalism is a political fact.' Two Premiers, twenty-five years apart, identical elemental word pictures, different continents. The start and the finish of dismantling an Empire.

Some historians have suggested that Neville Chamberlain pursued his appeasement policies to the point of disaster in the hope that Hitler and the Nazis would turn eastward and engage in a war with Stalin and the Communists until they mutually destroyed each other and thus the British Empire might have been preserved intact. History would argue that the idea made sense, for Britain indeed only became a great Imperial power by avoiding entanglements in Europe—and only became a second-class power when she forgot the lesson of history and tried to be a European power instead. Hitler, as late as 1940, would have negotiated peace which would have saved the Empire from disintegration but for Churchill, who was by then Prime Minister. Both plausible theories. In this context it is worth recalling that Churchill, who had always a romantic emotional conception of the British Raj and the future of the Empire's civilising mission among the subject races, never contemplated for a moment that the curtain on the grandeur of Britain's role in the world was about to come down forever. In 1937 he said: 'Of course my ideal is limited and narrow. I want to see the British Empire preserved for a few more generations in its strength and splendour.' That was when he was agonising over Baldwin's concessions to Indian nationalism led by Gandhi, 'that naked fakir' in Winston's phrase again. In his victory broadcast to the British people and the world on 13 May, 1945, he said: '. . . The British Commonwealth and Empire stands more united and more effectively powerful than at any time in its long romantic history.' And when he was Prime Minister he warned those agitating for freedom and independence in the Colonial countries that he had 'not become the Crown's First Minister in order to preside over the liquidation of the British Empire.'

GOEBBELS' PROGNOSIS
The irony is that Churchill's hated adversary, Josef Geobbels, Hitler's Propaganda Minister for fifteen years, showed a greater prescience about the break-up of the British Empire which would follow the collapse of the Third Reich—and showed a clearer vision, too, of what would happen to much of Europe under the Russian Communists. In his diaries written in the final weeks and months of the Third Reich he saw the end of the road for Britain too: 'Britain will have very little say in whatever may be happening in Europe in twenty-five to thirty years' time'; 'Shortly after the end of the War Churchill will be despatched to the wilderness'; 'Churchill has been condemned by fate to put Bolshevism in the saddle in Europe'; 'The British people will lose whatever happens'.* The cruel irony was that the British Empire's final and perilous collapse was more accurately foreseen by the doomed men in Hitler's bunker than by anyone at the top in London where everyone expected a speedy return to the Imperial pomp and plumes of the 1930s. Goebbels used the phrase 'The Iron Curtain' twelve months before Winston Churchill's Fulton speech.

Thus we said goodbye to all our Imperial yesterdays.

* *The Goebbels Diaries*. Edited by Hugh Trevor-Roper (Secker and Warburg).

4

ECLIPSE OF THE TWO ELITES

By far the greatest revolution between the Parliament of the early thirties and today's Parliament as we approach the eighties has been in the character and structure of the Tory and Labour Parties at Westminster. The MPs of the thirties on both sides of the House not only reflected the Imperial world-wide interests but embodied a stability, continuity and identity of their own, each with a specialised class character. Each party had its special stamp, image and tradition, displayed in the majority of cases by clothes and accents, whereas today the journalist trying to identify the newcomers in the lobbies after a general election finds that the modern Tory and Labour intakes are indistinguishable from each other in vowels, suits, even school ties and universities. The old identities have disappeared. The contemporary MPs, irrespective of parties, come from a narrow social base, overwhelmingly middle class. It is not that Parliament has become classless. The explanation is that the old class identities are no longer represented. The historic family names among the aristocrats, born to rule and lead by centuries of breeding and experience, have gone. So also have the great anchormen of the Labour Party, inspired by faith, vision, and class and family loyalties. Instead we have a mass of centrist neutralism of the middle, basically the same, where it is difficult to determine one from the other.

In the sociological jargon more fashionable today the Conservative and Labour Parties have lost their former class elitism. This may account for the impression that at moments of high pressure in modern conditions, even if the global scope of the crises has been scaled down to the domestic, the parties appear to have less stability, and are more excitable in their zest for instant reaction and instant phrasing of solutions, disciplined and polished in short sentences for instant TV consumption. Loyalties are more fluid and less solidly based.

In short, what has happened in my lifetime is the total eclipse of the old ruling classes, which provided both parties with their leadership and anchors—for Labour then had its ruling elite just as powerfully established as were the Tories in their social class. By comparison both parties are now significantly rootless, notably because they have lost their old links leading directly to and from their old area and territorial power groupings, the true source of their former missions and identities.

First, in trying to recapture the image of the old Conservative Party that has totally disappeared, the best starting point is to identify the power and influence of the old titled land-owning families, in a vast majority of cases dedicated to public service over many centuries and trained from birth for the Westminster course, first for the Commons hurly-burly and later in life for the Lordly pastures. There were twenty-three MPs who were heirs to peerages of senior status and highest quality ermine when I started observing the Westminster scene. The list is reproduced here in detail because it reveals the widely based territorial nature of the Conservative Party then and what has been wiped out by the zeal for mass uniformity:

MP	Constituency	Peerage
Lord Apsley	Bristol C.	Earl Athurst
Lord Balniel	Lonsdale	Earl of Crawford
Viscount Borodale	Peckham	Earl Beatty
Lord Burghley	Peterborough	Marquis of Exeter
Viscount Castlereagh	Down	Marquis of Londonderry
Viscount Cranborne	Dorset S.	Marquis of Salisbury
Marquis of Clydesdale	Renfrew E.	Duke of Hamilton
Earl of Dalkeith	Roxburgh	Duke of Buccleuch
Lord Dunglass	Lanark	Earl of Home
Viscount Elmley	Norfolk E.	Earl of Beauchamp
Marquis of Hartington	Derbyshire W.	Duke of Devonshire
Captain Hope	Aston, B'ham	Lord Rankellour
L. R. Lumley	York	Earl of Scarbrough
Viscount Lymington	Basingstoke	Earl of Portsmouth
J. P. Maclay	Paisley	Lord Maclay
T. Hall-Caine	Wavertree	Lord Brocket
W. Ormsby-Gore	Stafford	Lord Harlech
C. Rhys	Guildford	Lord Dynevor
Lord Scone	Perth	Earl of Mansfield
Lord Stanley	Fylde	Earl of Derby
Marquis of Tichfield	Newark	Duke of Portland
Viscount Weymouth	Frome	Marquis of Bath
Viscount Wolmer	Aldershot	Earl of Selborne

These were all the first male born, in line to succeed to the broad acres, the famous castles and noble piles. Second and subsequent sons also sought careers at Westminster. A few names only need be mentioned to illustrate the continuity. Captain James Stuart, second son of the Earl of Moray, was MP for Moray and Nairn and subsequently a Cabinet Minister (before starting his own line as the first Viscount Stuart of Findhorn); Lord Colm Crichton-Stuart, third son of the Marquis of Bute, who sat for one of the Bute family's territorial seats; Oliver Stanley, a younger son of the Earl of Derby, who had all the brain and personality to become party leader but for his untimely death; and many others.

The roll-call of these famous families and historic titles prompts the inevitable jokes and barbs about these seats being the last of the pocket boroughs available as of right, to be presented as gift-offerings ordained at birth to the heirs of the Dukes, Marquises and Earls to do a stint in the Commons before being called to higher things among their more natural equals in the Lords. Unquestionably the system produced abuse of patronage, especially in the more fashionable county seats which were slower to catch up with modern democracy and the compulsory demands for middle-class egalitarianism and uniformity. But much profounder factors were involved than jokes about 'the first of the litter' (Lloyd George at his best). The demands of public duty and the calls of service to the community were also a compulsive factor, bred in the bone. With but few exceptions the heirs lived in the constituencies they served. They were linked and identified with their home communities. Inevitably snobbery and ingrained deference in county districts to titles and castles were factors in tipping the balance when selection conferences were held. Even so, I hazard the guess without risk of libel or defamation that the majority of modern newcomers who fell heir to the old county seats as they were vacated by old families are not so sensitively tuned to the ideals of public life and national concern as their predecessors.

The Parliamentary reference book, *Dod's Parliamentary Companion*, used to devote a page to printing the constituency and family details of MP heirs to peerages. But when the list became zero the idea of publishing a blank page did not appeal to the editors, so the practice was scrapped when the end of the lordly road was reached.

RETREAT OF TITLED GENTRY

Where have the contemporary heirs to the rolling shires and historic castles gone, the young men who will be the Dukes, Marquises, Earls and the like in the twenty-first century? A random cross-check of the present incumbents of the honorific titles of breeding and gallantry produces a variety of reasons. Many of the first-born males from the ermine and purple have found richer rewards in the City, lending their names to merchant banks, multi-national conglomerates who like the polish of the old aristocracy to add lustre to the boardroom: the big money-spinners in advertising, public relations and the entertainment worlds have picked up the odd Duke or Marquis of the future for their letter-heads; show business and the pop world of entertainment, boutiques, groups and galleries get their quota. Also conducting visitors round their historic homes earns bigger money more rapidly than trudging, like their fathers did, through the Westminster division lobbies. And, of course, in this democratic age, local selection committees are afraid that titles have lost their sparkle as vote-catchers, when middle-class mediocrity may have a stronger pulling power.

It was not only by blue blood that the old-style Conservative Party was distinguished in the inter-war years. When I first graced the Westminster scene there were other substantial features appropriate to the period which have long since gone. First, on the Tory benches, there were 125 knights and baronets, not admittedly scions of historic families which had helped to run the country for centuries but nevertheless who had broken through the social barrier. Perhaps some of them did fit Stanley Baldwin's description of hard-faced types who had done well out of the First World War and considered that a knighthood here and a baronetcy there (where they had failed to make the peerage in one bound) recognised the arrival of the new monied classes. But in my recollection, confirmed by research, the big majority were men who had served their country on active service in the trenches in the First World War, and followed that up by another two decades of constant infantry life parading through the Westminster lobbies.

These knights and 'barts' of the shires provided much natural rich material for the young scribes and pharisees in the temple like myself, who moved around as unbelievers in the holy places. To a unique extent, however, they provided bottom and anchor and character to an extent that the modern young Tories fail to produce close on half-a-century later.

THE HONOURS SYSTEM

In the thirties knighthoods and baronetcies were part of the political system, part of the patronage set-up which nobody dreamt of concealing. Twice a year these honours came up with the rations which used to be eagerly awaited and devoured in the front line of politics. The point of the so-called honours system blatantly exploited by Lloyd George with so much hearty and cynical enjoyment was not that he was selling titles for good money, it was that he was such a practised poacher in the Tories' preserve, and had bagged or bought so many choice and coveted birds of paradise on which the Tory Whips had set their eyes for handsome cheques for party funds. So the Conservatives had much leeway to make up and the Birthday and New Year lists invariably included six to eight MPs knighted, or if already in that state, moved a step higher to baronetcy as a reward for past good behaviour and a stimulus to them to beget heirs of their own to whom the 'bart' would pass in a new hereditary line. It was part of the system. The rules were clearly understood. An MP became an hon. treasurer to this or that back-bench committee of MPs, the next year an extra stripe would be earned on becoming secretary, then after a spell in this role as linkman with the Chief Whip, the deputy chairmanship beckoned. Then a year in the chair followed, to be crowned at the end of the procession with the title. The entire process was gone through with the stately movements of a Victorian quadrille. If anyone proved too rebellious he would be tipped off over a late night Scotch by one of the Whips that because he had proved to be a bit of a bounder in the mess, with disloyal conduct unbecoming to an officer and gentleman, he might have to go back to the end of the queue. And his darling lady wife, who was such a charming hostess, would not like that, would she? (I was shown privately by an irreverent party executive a list of MPs who had written in for knighthoods for themselves. In each case one reason was quoted: 'It's nothing to me, of course, you know that, only it would mean so very much to my dear wife who has suffered in loneliness during all these all-night sittings!')

The Conservative Party I knew in the early thirties comprised not only twenty-three heirs to famous titles earmarking them for the Lords, and 125 knights and baronets mentioned above, it also comprised 128 officers who used service ranks, most of them Majors and above right up to divisional, corps and army commanders (and similar ranks in the other two Services including a couple of Admirals). There was also a complement of younger Members who had been Captains on active service. The importance of these men in influencing the nation's destiny throughout the twenties and thirties has too often been overlooked in the endless histories of the period. They were not honorary officers, holding courtesy ranks. With few exceptions they had been combatants in Flanders trenches and in the front lines in other war fronts. While many of them had been in the Guards, my records confirm that a substantial majority had been on active service with their county regiments; they had not only seen the carnage in the trenches but had commanded the men from their home battalions in much bloody fighting and had had the depressing task of writing letters of condolence to the mothers and wives of the men who had died under their command on the battlefield. They were the survivors of the decimated generation and had personal ties of bravery and friendship with the ex-soldiers in their own regiments and the bereaved families in their constituencies, for they had fought and suffered together; that was a precious relationship that could not be bequeathed to the new generation of MPs.

This background is of the highest relevance to understanding what the Conservative Party of the twenties and thirties was all about: the heirs to historic titles, the knights and baronets of the shires, the officers who had commanded men and machines in many bloody battles, represented the Tory Party's ethos to an extent impossible to equal by today' generation of Tories. They were the party's *roots*, from the *grassroots*. Between seventy and eighty per cent had their permanent family homes in their constituencies, their families lived there among their constituents, and did not require any of the modern complexities of opinion poll sampling or market surveys to know what their people back home were thinking.

TORIES OLD AND NEW

Just to complete the comparative studies of then and now, between the day before yesterday and today, contemporary statistics disclose that few of the current Conservative members have traditional or family ties with their constituencies or shared the community life in the services in training camp or on active service. Some indeed have moved into their seats to be more accessible for weekend surgeries, but few have personal roots in the seats they represent. As part of the increasing demands of ever more professionalism in politics this may be an inevitable trend. Even so, it is largely peculiar to British politics and is contrary to the accepted American pattern which continues to prevail even today; in the United States anyone with political ambition stands no chance if he does not seek minor office first in his home town or home community, progressing in due course to higher office in his home State as the essential base.

To complete the Conservative profile with a few comparative details from today's statistics: there are only 8 heirs to major or minor titles, there are only 23 knights and 'barts' on the Tory benches (the long breaks imposed by Labour Governments broke the flow of twice-annual allotments), and only 2 use military rank—inevitable as we draw farther away from 1945.

The old Conservative Party with its historic mission, ideals, traditions, beliefs and land-owning character really died at the 1945 general election. An entire generation of famous families, squires, officers, leaders of major industries, the land, services, and Empire, were wiped out, never to be reproduced. Over 130 Tory MPs were defeated, another 90 (the survivors from the twenties and thirties) retired. So getting on for 230 MPs, about three-quarters of an entire party, disappeared in one day and with them went the Conservatives' clearly defined traditions and beliefs. The magnitude of the party's loss of the pre-war Conservatives is brought home when it is remembered that the total voting strength of the Tories after the second 1974 elections was 276. Today's replacements provide notable comparisons in the Party's composition and character. Close on fifty per cent are classed as businessmen (none of them former captains of industry, who used to be so prominent; instead they are of lower to mid-tier management), the number from the professions has dropped by over twelve per cent, lawyers represent the strongest single profession, with 60 and a surprisingly high number of journalists, 22; while directors of large and small firms total 72. That is the modern profile which displaced the traditional character.

The Conservatives were not alone in this special identity with the elitism of rulers and leaders drawn from clearly defined social backgrounds, of class, rank, acres and privilege. The Labour Party of the thirties was equally distinguishable by its own power groupings of class and public service elitism which gave it counterbalancing features which were just as strongly pronounced and powerfully entrenched. These were the mutual features which gave the period such a special character and stability, features which cannot be identified in either party today. Indeed, both the Tory and Labour Parties have become very much more rootless than were the parties I knew first close on a half-century ago. It is not that they have simply responded to social, educational and economic changes, potent as these have proved. It is more that they are cut off from the traditional forces in the nation which gave them their idealism and purpose. They have both been cut adrift from their old anchors and moorings which gave them bottom and stability in the far bigger political and world storms of the period. Which explains why politics have become more 'fluid and mobile', the pundits' fashionable phrase to account for instability and uncertainty whenever the going becomes stormy.

The vast transformation in the make-up of the Conservative Party has thus been balanced by an equally far-reaching upheaval in the character of the Labour Party since that time. The Conservatives may have had their elite of historic titled families but Labour had its special elitist roll-call of Lord Mayors and Mayors, who gave the party not merely its special character and experience of public life but at the same time represented its bedrock foundations in the communities. The lesson is that a powerful and influential grouping of able men possessed a mountain of first-hand experience *before* they ever became Parliamentary candidates and reached Westminster.

LABOUR'S PEDIGREE

Labour's roll of honour was just as impressive and influential as that of the Tories. Prime Minister Attlee was in local government for many years

71

before becoming Mayor of Stepney and later the borough's MP; Herbert Morrison, Deputy Prime Minister, was likewise Mayor of his home area of Hackney and later leader of the London County Council before reaching Westminster as MP for the borough (and 'MP for London' because of his LCC base). These were the two most notable examples, but there were a great many other leaders who played a notable part in the development of the Labour Party in the inter-war years who operated from powerful regional bases. Among them were David Adams (Consett, Durham), who had been Lord Mayor of Newcastle; David Morgan Adams (Mayor of Poplar); William Green, Mayor of Deptford; Valentine McEntee, Mayor of Walthamstow; Fred Marshall, Lord Mayor of Sheffield; Fred Simpson, Lord Mayor of Leeds; Will Thorne, Mayor of West Ham. No carpet-baggers there.

Their names may not mean much to the new generation, but there were thirty-two other Labour MPs in the author's first Parliament in the thirties who had spent many years on borough and county councils and had been chairmen of the education and housing committees for years before becoming Mayors and Lord Mayors and then MPs; indeed, in a large number of cases they combined local government with Westminster careers (in the days when membership of the local council often involved loss of earnings, unlike today's expenses and emoluments). Four of Labour's future Cabinet Ministers were in this category: J. R. Clynes, Home Secretary; Arthur Greenwood, Deputy Leader and Lord President; Chuter Ede, Home Secretary and Education Secretary, and Jack Lawson, War Minister. In addition, there were twelve full-time general secretaries or executive presidents of major trade unions in the Commons. Indeed, most of the influential TUC General Council members were at Westminster too.

The TUC's elite combined with the Labour Party's elite from Westminster, town hall and county hall provided the Labour Party with an elitist power system, which, like the Tories' own traditional groupings, reinforced the party with stability and roots. Today's rootlessness, without personal ties with the local communities, is peculiar to the new English style. It is not, for example, experienced in the United States, as mentioned above, nor among our new partners in the Common Market—particularly in Germany and France, while in Switzerland the Canton system reinforces regional, religious and language identities.

What strikes me most of all is that both parties have lost their old provincial base, identity and independence. At the same time as Labour has lost their race of leaders in the towns, cities and counties who used to exert a special influence and identity on Government and party, the Tories too have lost their old regional dynasties, and the independent reserves of

72

power and authority which the Chamberlains displayed in Birmingham, the Stanleys in Lancashire, the Salvidge rule in Liverpool; these old dynasties have been grabbed by the central party bureaucracy in Smith Square in the name of progress and reorganisation. So instead of tough political slogging in the big provincial cities the ambitious young Tories have perfected a short cut to get on selection lists, it does not matter where. They first get on to the Central Office staff, do work for the Conservative Political Centre, the Research Department and other Central Committees of the party; in no time at all they reach the candidates' list maintained at Central Office and are in the best position to get the push of patronage necessary to be included in the selection lists for good seats. That's the secret: start at the centre and work outwards, and avoid the sweated labour entailed the other way round.

Similar short cuts are also fashionable in the modern Labour Party. Instead of slogging for years in the council chamber of the home town and establishing a reputation for public work, the ambitious young Labour aspirants come fresh from university and college to find their own quick routes. The best formula seems to become an adviser on policies, ideas and speech forms to a Departmental Minister, with the status of temporary civil servant, or become an activist on the teaching staff at some college, polytechnic, school or training college; or, especially rewarding, make a name as a difficult radical type in the media. The formula saves a lot of drudgery on councils and local community jobs. And a delicate Marxist colouring helps to shorten the journey. Three sets of figures tell the story of what has replaced the old status of mayors and local authorities members in the modern party; there are over eighty Labour MPs classed as teachers and lecturers, nearly fifty lawyers, and, surprisingly, twenty-seven journalists of undistinguished status.

There was very little Marxism noticeable inside the Labour Party in the thirties, despite the fact that Communism created a glamour of its own in the days of depression. The most striking feature of the far left of the period was that the Communists and Marxists were kept to such a minor role because the Independent Labour Party, the most militant movement, was powerfully anti-Communist. It was only when the ILP lost its power that the Marxists started to capture Labour's left. The Bevanites of the fifties were in the ILP tradition. It was more recently in the Tribunites that the Marxists gained influence. Morgan Phillips, who was secretary at Transport House for many years up to his premature death, once said that Labour owed more to Methodism than to Marxism. There was visible evidence all around me when I started lobbying at Westminster. The Christian Socialist group were powerful and influential. Their leaders were men of the cloth, with three Free Church ministers in

73

the House: Rev. James Barr (Coatbridge), Rev. R. Sorensen (Leyton) and Rev. G. S. Wood (Finsbury), and many lay preachers as well. They met as an active group every week, not at prayer meetings seeking converts, but as politicians who were practising Christians anxious to discuss among themselves not the fine print of party policies but the morality and quality of the latest policies in human and social terms. The eclipse of this influence inside Labour by the departed Methodism and Presbyterianism illustrates another substantial change in the texture and structure of politics in these years.

There are few men and women around at Westminster today who have spent much of their time in the local council chamber. The paradox is that the opposite trend has gathered strength in France. In the present National Assembly there are sixty-eight mayors of towns with populations of more than 30,000, with an even greater number from smaller communities. In France local service is the usual if not inevitable passport to Parliament—as in the United States—and with the decline in the rôle of Parliament in Paris greater importance is attached to careers in local authorities where roots remain strong. This plurality of mandates has its obvious drawbacks, but it does give French local government a status, priority and power which the British system has lost by cutting the old roots, with fewer direct links left between the Commons Chamber and the Mayor's Parlour.

TODAY'S PAROCHIAL OUTLOOK

In the thirties Parliament had at its disposal much more experience of the world than is discernible among today's Ministers and MPs. It was then packed with men with first-hand knowledge of the Dominions, Colonies and foreign countries not only because they had served in front-line service in battle but as the result of the constant cross-fertilisation between Westminster and the executive and administrative services all over the world. Not merely were the best among MPs frequently posted abroad as Governors and on similar missions—John Buchan (the first Lord Tweedsmuir) who went from the Commons as Governor-General of Canada is a notable example—but men who had served in the Imperial and Colonial Services all over the world often became MPs at the end of their overseas careers. By far the outstanding example in this group in my time was Sir John Anderson (later the first Lord Waverley). He had first been a Whitehall career civil servant, ending up as Permanent Secretary at the Home Office; then he was Under-Secretary in Ireland during the crisis years of the early twenties and was later Governor of Bengal. When this mission was completed he became a back-bench independent MP for the Scottish Universities and later a senior Cabinet Minister in the Chamberlain and Churchill Governments. There were many others at Westminster in the same pattern of service, though not of the formidable calibre of Anderson. This background of global experience is no longer at Westminster's disposal, nor of course are the opportunities to acquire it. Today's MPs are limited to being chosen by the Whips for courtesy overseas jaunts or delegations as their main hope of seeing anything beyond their native shores, usually for a week or two only. In career terms, the EEC at Brussels offers the main scope for a few. But there are few Andersons, Buchans and others of their stature around the Westminster parish today.

The massive transformation sketched in this chapter in the old traditional character and composition of the two major parties exposes the great paradox of modern politics. As the Tories lost their old aristocratic, class, county, and school identities and Labour lost their old aristocracy of power by the eclipse of the generation of mayors, regional leaders, and trade union bosses, the two parties grew more alike in class backgrounds, education, accents, clothes, standards. But these similarities are top dressing only. While blue blood is very scarce, there is not a calloused hand in sight. But there are today, and the 1980s will increasingly confirm this, deeper ideological differences between the two parties than ever existed in the thirties. And with less tolerance and mutual respect. The more alike the identikits and profiles of the parties have become the more bitter and widely separated in political basics and humanities have they grown.

5

RAPE OF THE MOTHER OF PARLIAMENTS

In my lifetime's career as a newspaperman I have lived through, and helped to report as part of unfolding daily history, a greater world upheaval, measured in human, technological and power terms, than in many preceding centuries bracketed together. Nowhere has this transformation taken place at greater speed and with more fundamental consequences for the material well-being and human happiness of much of the rest of the world than on our front doorstep at Westminster. From my advance observation post in Parliament and Whitehall I have witnessed a long succession of historic changes, many of which have brought great blessings to mankind in civilised values and in national aspirations. The Last Post and the Piper's Lament for Imperial glory have long since sounded. The White Commonwealth and more than three dozen former Colonies have sought and found their own new destinies. Now the European Economic Commission in Brussels and its vast bureaucracy, more formidable and autocratic than anything known in Whitehall during the old Colonial regime, has already removed a large sector of power from London. The new European Assembly (at Strasbourg and Luxembourg), with directly elected MPs, and the possible Assemblies for Scotland and Wales will mean deprivation of yet more power and authority from Westminster. Yet at the very heart of this enormous transformation in world status, the only institution which has carried on, deaf and blind to change all around it, yet with its role more and more circumscribed, is the British Parliament.

The Parliament I leave at the end of the journey is much more inbred, introspective, impotent and self-centred than it was when I first appeared on the scene. After saying farewell to Imperial cares and surrendering so much to the EEC, Westminster by now should have readjusted to its new role in the world and prepared to become the most compact, streamlined, modernised and efficient Assembly in the world, capitalising on centuries of experience. But successive Parliaments and Governments have dis-

76

played an obstinate resistance to modern change and reform. Dozens and dozens of Royal Commissions and official inquiries have been set up over the years to reorganise and modernise professions and industries—such as the Press, BBC and ITA, the law, doctors and countless others—but never one for Parliament to get Westminster in tune for the eighties and beyond. There have been an impressive number of Select and Procedure Committees over the years but their reports, when selectively adopted, have meant only tinkering first-aid repairs and trifling cosmetic adjustments.

YESTERDAY, TODAY AND TOMORROW

As we enter the eighties we still find that identical procedures, rules, and practices are, broadly speaking, unchanged from those of the thirties. One's parting impression is not of the scale and importance of reforms and improvements carried out during the past half-century, but of the magnitude of what has endured unchanged. Indeed, Parliament is almost as it was a century ago when my predecessor, Sir Alexander Mackintosh, journeyed from Aberdeen to Westminster in 1881 when the Press Gallery and Parliamentary Press Lobby were first opened to the Press outside London. It is an astonishing record of the same yesterday, today, tomorrow and forever, especially when in future the effective limit of its realm will be restricted by the English Channel.

While all this is only too true in geographical, physical and procedural terms, in power and democratic terms the position is even more sombre and ominous. The Westminster Parliament today exercises less effective power than ever. In one man's life-time it has surrendered substantial authority and control to the Executive, the generic term for that marriage of convenience between Government and the Civil Service. This is an unholy alliance which has become the most powerful dynasty in the free world.

PMs AND PRESIDENTS

There has been much speculation among academics who study such developments from the outside about whether British Prime Ministers have become more Presidential in style. Those whose job it has been to report at first hand contemporary events as they unfold every day in Washington and London are under no illusions. Prime Ministers have in fact become more powerful than even Presidents. They are less exposed to the constant checks and balances of the American system which frequently pose more formidable problems for the President in getting controversial measures through Congress than the Premier in the Whitehall-Westminster network.

The irony is that this revolution which has transferred power from what used to be regarded as the altar of democracy at Westminster to the secret corridors of Whitehall has not happened by sudden stealth. It has a long history of growth. It was first pin-pointed over a half-century ago by Lord Hewart, the Lord Chief Justice. As LCJ he was one of the pillars of the Establishment, but even he was appalled and scared by what he saw in close-up from the inside. He wrote a remarkable book on *The New Despotism* to alert Parliament and the country to the dangerous new trend then starting. Few sentences are sufficient to tell his story: the new tyranny he saw taking place as 'the accumulation of despotic power in the hands of anonymous officials'; 'the pretensions and encroachments of the bureaucracy—the new despotism'; and 'the departmental policy of secrecy, which is inveterate, is in itself sufficient to condemn the system under which the public departments act as tribunals to decide disputes of a judicial nature'. That was how the deflowering of Parliament started all those years ago, when Britain was at the apogee of her power. But the process gathered speed and scope after the Second World War. When the curtain came down finally on the great Imperial drama Parliament, in theory, should have been left with more time to devote to running the shop at home. But not so. The rout has proved even more total than Hewart's grim warnings. There is, overwhelmingly, much greater secrecy in Whitehall and less openness in Government. All the time the growth of bureaucracy has been phenomenal. Britain at the height of her Imperial power ran the world-wide show from London with 128,000 civil servants. At the latest count, in her new home-orientated status, the total was 564,000 (non-industrial, of course)—and still growing.

The fashionable theory to explain this vast filching of power is to suggest that Prime Ministers and their Cabinets are like putty in the hands of Whitehall's mandarins, the dupes of clever men. This is too plausible. In my case-book Premiers are the eager allies of the formidable corps of Permanent Secretaries who constitute probably the most impressive battery of brain-power concentration anywhere in the world with the exception of the French system. For the greater the power acquired and deployed by them both in the cross-bred Executive the better it suits the Prime Ministers, liberated as they are from a troublesome Parliament forever reminding them about its paramountcy.

THE NEW ESTABLISHMENT

The process has grown steadily, like the inevitability of gradualness. The first five of the dozen Prime Ministers in my gallery were punctiliously constitutionalist in their deference to and recognition of Britain being a Parlimentary democracy. Lloyd George and Churchill were brought up in the Parliamentary as distinct from the Whitehall tradition, and to this extent their respect for and deference to Westminster was inbred and instinctive. The other Prime Ministers between the wars were frequently their own Leaders of the House of Commons (the high office of Lord President is more often than not identified nowadays with the supra-Chief Government Whip as Commons Leader). Baldwin spent many hours every week sitting listening to back-bench MPs in order to get a feel of what Parliament was really thinking. Chamberlain devoted great attention to keeping his influence over Westminster. MacDonald was acknowledged to be a superb Parliamentarian. Eden had been leader of the House for five years, which required his prolonged attendance. But latter-day Premiers perform their Question Time spots twice a week and then quickly disappear behind the Speaker's Chair, with few contacts with the mass of MPs. Most Ministers make a bolt for their Departments immediately after they have done their set pieces on the Front Bench. Time-and-motion study would come up with the evidence that modern Prime Ministers and the senior Cabinet Ministers devote more time nowadays to meetings with the two new pillars of the Establishment, the Trades Union Congress and the Confederation of British Industries than they do with the Commons and MPs—for the simple reason that Prime Ministers do not feel under any pressure to pay much attention to Parliament so long as it rubber-stamps what is put before it.

Parliament has co-operated, apart from an occasional whimper, in sacrificing its authority and power. My conviction is that the pre-war Parliaments kept a much firmer control over Governments and Whitehall because of a combination of factors which no longer exist. There was very much more independence inside *all* the parties then. Now the Whips and, through them, the central party machines are much more authoritarian. For the Executive bug has also affected the party hierarchies, who find it easier to identify themselves with the Executive, the TUC and the CBI than with Parliament in real power terms. The party machines, like the other two bodies mentioned, have become very much more dictatorial and centralised; each in turn has lost its old regional roots in the formerly independent area dynasties. This is in harmony with what has been happening in industries and commerce, forever growing more powerfully corporate and multi-national in organisation. It is not only in Whitehall that bureaucracy flourishes in profusion.

The reality is that the modern Parliament has become in practice a central registry for recording votes and giving effect to decisions taken elsewhere in the Cabinet and in Government Departments. Parliament now governs only in the technical formal sense. Indeed, party meetings have become more important in most instances than the debates in the Commons, because so strong is the measure of authority and discipline now vested in the party machines that once decisions are taken at such meetings, in the Labour Party in particular, these become mandatory, to be obeyed subsequently in the chamber.

Many factors have combined to account for this impotence of Parliament. The total collapse of Empire started the rot. Three major constitutional measures have transferred vast powers to Brussels, Strasbourg, and Luxembourg. We are only at the start of this process. As their appetites and ambitions grow, as inevitably they will grow, less will be left to Westminster. When Edward Heath as Prime Minister offered in critical days at No. 10 Downing Street to share major economic decisions with the TUC and the CBI he really spelled out the reality of the new power empires which participate in the great decisions and consultations with the Executive, overshadowing and by-passing Parliament. Premiers and their Ministers and Whitehall's top brass talk more freely to the CBI and TUC about how their minds are working on major issues than they would ever dream of doing to MPs and the Lobby. (See Chapter 9, 'The Lobby'.)

A new generation of top civil servants now run Whitehall who never knew what the supremacy of Parliament used to mean in terms of power and the wielding of it. Despite fairy tales about more open Government and decision-sharing in order to create an informed democracy, not only are the average citizens more defenceless than their fathers and grandfathers were, but secrecy is tougher and more complete. MPs know less, and are told less, than the preceding generations about what is going on behind the scenes. This is true of political and media correspondents too.

MPs have mostly themselves to blame for the fact that they are no longer treated by the Executive—and indeed by public opinion—as significant and influential people. The pretence that they exert any noticeable power over events is no longer taken seriously. Constituency parties, through their selection committees, are not conspicuously successful in finding potential men of destiny.

THE OLD BACK-BENCHES
When I first became a political correspondent the House of Commons was dominated by substantial personalities. I refer not only to the great historical figures like Lloyd George and Winston Churchill who not merely dominated Parliament and their Governments but who enjoyed world-wide reputations and influence in and out of office. There were many other outstanding men on the back-benches who had national and international reputations. To mention a few: Sir Austen Chamberlain, Sir Robert Horne, Walter Runciman, Sir John Simon, followed later by

Anthony Eden, Duff Cooper, and the young generation of Tory rebels like Harold Macmillan and Robert Boothby. MPs were much less susceptible to Whip-management. There was much more independence on both sides of the House. The Liberal Party was markedly stronger than to-day, even after the Asquith-Lloyd George split, and acted as the focus and rallying point for Tory and Labour rebels. Most of all, the strong mood of independence was fortified by the presence of a dozen Independent MPs representing the Universities. They were figures of great substance: John Buchan, A. P. Herbert, Eleanor Rathbone, Sir Arthur Salter; and Sir John Anderson just a year or so later. They were great independent campaigners: Miss Rathbone inspired the system of family allowances, A. P. Herbert introduced divorce reform. All these varied factors, among several others, combined to remind all Governments that their power and survival derived directly from Parliament. Unlike to-day, nobody forgot it.

The inexperience of the new generation of MPs of life in the outside world, where they never attained any positions of reponsibility, status or substance *before* reaching Westminster, makes it that much easier for Prime Ministers and the Executive to get their own way. This is in sharp contrast to the inter-war years when many outstanding personalities reached Westminster *after* having established their reputations as leaders in other fields (see Chapter 4). Now the preoccupation of party managers is to find promising young men from mid-tier management and professional careers for Westminster before they have had time to acquire experience, status and bottom elsewhere. Governments, in addition, used to have to watch their step with the back-benches on both sides which were strong in former Ministers who knew the ropes and were anxious to get back into office. Today the former Ministers still around are mainly misfits or discards who are of little account. Most ex-Ministers disappear immediately to the Lords, collecting the ermine as a bonus to their pensions.

If there were reasonable prospects that future intakes of new MPs might arrest the recent decline there might be greater hopes that somehow Westminster might claw back some of the crucial powers which have been grabbed by Whitehall in a conspiracy of mutual co-operation with Governments. Talent scouts and head-hunters anxious to organise future sources of potential leaders for the upper echelons may face bigger problems than have yet been identified. It is on the cards that the best material of the next generation of young English men and women from industry, business and the professions will respond with ambition to the glittering prizes offered by Brussels, Strasbourg and Luxembourg. They are less likely to respond to the challenge of the English dimension. The most promising young Scots of all parties are likely to prefer election to an Edinburgh Assembly, where they will be able to combine public service with private careers outside politics than trying their luck at St. Stephen's down South. This point for Scotland is pertinent. Both Labour and Tory Parties have to work very hard to discover anyone suitable to hold down the job of Scottish Secretary in the Cabinet. I recall pre-war Governments where there were six or seven Scots in their Cabinets. Since then the well has run dry. The same problem of choice confronts the best young Welsh of the future. Where will the Lloyd Georges and Aneurin Bevans seek political power and influence? If the most brilliant young men and women of the coming generations prefer the challenge of public careers in Europe will it be possible for Westminster to attract promising candidates? Obviously, if high-flyers go elsewhere and the second choices opt for Westminster, Parliament will never get any stronger. Thus the Executive will be left more impregnable than ever.

A BRIEF REVIVAL

Admittedly there were a few occasions in the past year or two when Parliament re-asserted some of its old independence and authority. The Government lost several crucial divisions on important policy issues. One or two Select Committees produced highly critical reports about Whitehall's dictatorship and the high-handed actions by senior civil servants. Hallelujahs were sung to the heavens. At last modern Governments were being sharply reminded that they are the servants and not the masters of Parliament and the nation. But these welcome instances reflected no real change of heart, or any radical variation in the balance of power concentrated overwhelmingly in the Executive. Instead they were due to the emergence of an entirely novel situation, a minority Government trying to function through a Parliament of minorities. Thus, in a much more mobile situation at Westminster a greater show of independence came to the front within and between *all* parties.

Because it was such a long time since Parliament breathed the heady air of independence and became aware for the first time for a generation that it could actually *control* a Government, and influence what the Government of the day could and could not do, nobody had any experience about how to operate and properly exploit the unusual position. So instead of a genuine effort by all sides to make the system work, the Government, the parties and the media saw every situation when the votes were to be on the knife-edge as an exciting crisis of confidence, over-played as a situation in danger of wrecking the constitution and leaving the country ungoverned and ungovernable. It was merely exciting scenes in political theatre. All because nobody could recall in modern times a

Government being in a situation where it was required and compelled to pay attention to what Parliament said.

The novel experience of having a minority Government in a house of minority parties oddly enough helped to create greater stability when it was realised that Parliament could be the top dog for a change. In short, the mood was there, the situation was right, but what was missing was the courage to follow through by embracing the ascendancy of Parliament as something of great value to be treasured for future guidance, and not just an exciting diversion in nightly arithmetic for the Whips, transient head-lines over the marmalade pot at breakfast, and a passing reference in the news bulletins.

One dreads to think what the 'New Despotism' will be like to live under by the end of the century if relief does not come in time to reverse the trends, because the Elective Dictatorship identified by Lord Hailsham will become even more sinister by virtue of the frightening scale of modern patronage forever being expanded.

PROPOSED CONGRESSIONAL-TYPE COMMITTEES

There is no single reform readily available which would by itself provide the miracle cure. The most hopeful and important of the many proposals that have been put forward was included in the report by the all-party Select Committee on Procedure in 1978. This recommended a well organ-ised new structure of Select Committees to scrutinise *all* activities of Government and Whitehall on behalf of the House of Commons, a dozen Committees in all, specialising in the main Departments of State. Prop-erly applied, with adequate staffing, the Committees would be able to start hauling back some of Parliament's old powers over the Executive and maintain a searching check on policies.

This would be getting closer to the American Committee system which deploys formidable power on behalf of the Congress over the President and the great Departments of State. Indeed, the chairmen of the Ameri-can Committees are such powerful figures that they have been described as power barons, exercising great influence over the White House and the major Departments in both executive and legislative policies. Theirs is a watchdog role, toughly inquisitorial, miniature legislatures within them-selves; and many of the chairmen are so well known, better known indeed than most of the President's Ministers, that they enjoy celebrity status on the national screen. Inevitably there would be some constitutional prob-lems in grafting most of the Congressional Committee system on to the older Westminster stock, but Washington emphatically points the way in which progress must be made.

Already at Westminster there are a few Committees of considerable influence, like the Committees on Expenditure, Public Accounts and European Legislation, which have proved of enormous importance in keeping Ministers and Civil Servants under surveillance and exposure. These successes owe much to the character and independence (as in Washington) of Committee chairmen, on both sides of the house: like Edward du Cann and Michael English, who have frequently shown great courage and indepedence. How would another twelve Committees empowered to keep the spotlight on separate Ministries be superimposed on the present Parliamentary system? Clearly, this would involve a major revolution. But one doubts whether the plan will ever make progress for one solid reason: the independence and critical faculties of the overwhelming mass of to-day's MPs are directly conditioned by the Whips, Government and Opposition alike. Government Whips' primary role in life is to ensure the survival of the Government on all occasions. And their starting point is to guarantee their Prime Minister and party masters that dangerous rebels are not to be tolerated, let alone encouraged. So MPs of the governing party will hesitate long before they sign reports which may conceivably injure their own Government or the individual reputations of the Prime Minister and members of the Cabinet of the day. Independence in politics has limited frontiers.

So one fears that the machines will prove too strong in the long term. Whips' discipline can be severe. MPs do not like to be passed over when promotions are going. The party system is very much less rigid and centralised in Washington: the greater flexibility and overlapping among parties in the United States fortifies the power of the Committee Chairmen; in any case, the President and his Ministers are in a more flexible relationship to the Senate and the House of Representatives than the Prime Minister is to Parliament.

Despite the misgivings of the purists more concerned over the theory of the *floor* of the Commons than with the need to reinforce the *structure* of Parliament, the extension of the Select Committee system, with emphatic powers in reserve to get all the facts they want from Ministers and Civil Servants, however elevated, holds out the main hope for reform and recovery. But it can only prove worth while if the leaderships and Whips on both sides are prepared to encourage greater independence by their MPs—and not to accuse members of traitorous betrayal any time they add their names to a critical document. Otherwise the system will be stultified, with the MPs peeling off on party lines signing minority and majority reports. Here patronage is powerful. MPs yearn for office. Courage is too often expendable when an office—however humble—at the disposal of the Prime Minister becomes available and when nominations are at the discretion of the Whips.

The Executive is always actively trying to extend its boundaries, at the same time reducing Parliament's powers to interfere, with 'We-Know-Best' plans of Whitehall. Not so long ago Mr Edward Short,* using his full authority as the then Lord President of the Council, Leader of the Commons, and Deputy Leader of the Labour Party in the Wilson Government, suggested a reform near and dear to his—and Whitehall's—heart. This was that a Government should have a series of Enabling Bills submitted to the Commons, with each Department lumping its policies in one broad statement of intent, leaving Ministers to fill in the details by Orders in Council! Surprisingly, I heard no cries of protest against this authoritarian lurch towards Government by decree. MPs did not raise even a whimper of protest at Mr Short's ideas to treat Parliament and members as rubber-stamps. Hitler, with his solution for the Reichstag, was ahead of his time!

In step with the vast powers of the State operated by Whitehall and its out-stations has been the growth of the menace of patronage, exploited openly as an instrument of Government by all Governments. This is the biggest and most dangerous growth industry in politics in my time. It is now on a scale which makes the abuses of patronage by earlier regimes, from Walpole onwards, seem small-time by comparison. In the United States the rewards ladled out by an incoming Administration, both in Washington and in individual States, to its supporters and backers are accepted as part of the system known as the gravy train or the pork barrel. Almost unnoticed the system has taken over in Britain too—but with less ostentation and without a whimper of protest. At the last count seven Cabinet Ministers have between them the patronage, or gift, of 4,233 jobs at their disposal, worth £4.2 million in perquisites. There are between 6,000 and 7,000 nominated posts paid at rates between £500 and £50,000-plus, with further perks thrown in. Recently the General Coun cil of the TUC had fourteen out of its thirty members nominated by Ministers as members of various State boards, all fee-paying jobs. One lucky fellow retired to become a part-time member of three different public bodies, at a gross salary exceeding his career pay. Government Departments are coy over giving the total of central and regional posts at their disposal, paid and unpaid, with expenses allowances thrown in; but one accurate estimate puts the total at between 30,000 and 50,000. Many of these belong to the army of the QUANGOS, described as the Quasi-Autonomous National & Government Officers, who exert considerable power and influence in a world of their own of State patronage. Yet this vast State apparatus of patronage has been created by Governments of all

* Later Lord Glenamara, chairman of Cable and Wireless.

parties with scant attention paid to its implications. As we saw in the Poulson, Dan Smith and Cunningham cases, the gap between patronage and corruption narrows noticeably when the temptations of the gravy train are around. It was Governor Earl Long of Louisiana who drew the distinction between himself and the notorious Huey; whereas Huey had always bought politicians, Earl had invariably found it more businesslike to hire them. The widespread operation of this vast new world of patronage as a built-in feature of the Executive's preferments and rewards must be classed as one of the most disturbing developments to become so firmly established during my years as an observer of how power is manipulated. Yet Parliament never debates how this complex world of patronage works. It is administered in general by the Executive as part of the system of by-passing Parliamentary scrutiny.

BLANKET OF SECRECY

One of the main obstacles to MPs acquiring any direct influence on policies before they reach their final shape is the impenetrable blanket of secrecy maintained by the Executive. This prevents members sharing in the prior process of consultation or participation in decision-forming. If members are never told the alternatives they remain ignorant of the processes of governing—and of course secrecy is essential to all Governments for this adds to the mystique of governing. MPs are the most uninformed people in public life. They are told less than political journalists about what is going on; their contacts with Whitehall are minimal; they are mostly ignorant of how Government works; they count on the media to tell them what's up and what's pending, what took place at today's Cabinet and what's in the pipeline for next week's meeting.

It suits the Government and Whitehall excellently to keep Parliament and the Press in the dark simultaneously, though separately, with controlled leaks to lighten the darkness. The failure of MPs of all parties and the media to co-operate in joint campaigns to break through the secrecy barriers, demanding more disclosure, more access to information, and more consultation, ensures the Executive a quieter life. The reasons for this dichotomy are of long standing. Throughout the centuries statesmen and politicians have never liked or trusted the Press, now widened to embrace TV and Radio. Frenetic campaigns about the evils of secret Government and the eternal verities of the freedom of the Press have too often been seen at Westminster as primarily Fleet Street gimmicks inspired by self-interest. Such strident campaigning has always played into the hands of the Government and Whitehall, because it is the oldest ploy in the business to balance the media and Lobby off against Parliament and the MPs. Hence the conspicuous success of the Executive in resisting the more excitable demands for modernising the Official Secrets Act in any major sense, as well as liberalising the laws on defamation, contempt, libel and the like. In this sector the Press has probably overplayed its hand by projecting the arguments as though the interests of the Press were paramount, whereas they are crucial only because they are basic to the nation's interests, which the Press and Parliament exist to represent and safeguard.

If such a common front were formed the consequent pressures from Parliament and Press pursuing identical demands for more openness, as well as closer Parliamentary involvement and scrutiny, would at the same time strengthen the hands inside Whitehall's walled city of those who are anxious to see reforms introduced. Indeed, two former Permanent Heads of the Civil Service were not merely ahead of their senior colleagues but in advance of the Prime Ministers and their Cabinets of the day by advocating greater disclosure. Sir William (later Lord) Armstrong advised his Permanent Secretaries to become more accessible to the media and the Lobby Correspondents (as indeed they were as a matter of course when I started in the business), even suggesting that they should consider taking lessons in how to cope with TV interviews. Nothing much came of the Armstrong initiative, mainly because some Ministers were not very keen on their Permanent Secretaries explaining Government policies to TV audiences and probably not stressing the political mix. His successor as Head of the Civil Service, Sir Douglas Allen (later Lord Croham), also recommended more disclosure of background papers to explain official policies, on the ground that such disclosure of the facts which influenced the final decisions would help to create good Government, political stability and moderation, as well as expanding an informed public opinion. But his successor, Sir Ian Bancroft, was not oversold on the proposal, because he feared that too open contacts with journalists might increase the risk of unauthorised disclosure.

This is unquestionably one of the basics in the Whitehall mind which triggers automatic reflexes. It has a long history. When Harold Macmillan was Prime Minister I invited Sir Norman Brook (later Lord Normanbrook), the Cabinet Secretary and Head of the Civil Service, to be my guest at a luncheon being given for the PM. His reply tells all, and is as relevant today as it was twenty years ago. This is how Sir Norman saw the dangers of contact with the untouchables:

> I have always thought it best that, in my capacity as Secretary of the Cabinet, I should avoid direct personal contact with the Press. I am conscious that, by following that principle, I have deprived myself of many pleasant contacts; but I believe that, even so, it has been the wisest course for me to follow. I realise that you may have asked me in my other capacity as Head of the Civil Ser-

vice; but I must take account of the fact that I still remain Secretary of the Cabinet. And, that being so, I feel I must ask you to excuse me. I am sorry to have to write like this.

A WRITTEN CONSTITUTION?

Many powerful voices have been raised demanding major reforms to challenge the serious dangers which have emerged as the result of the prolonged and spectacular decline in the paramountcy of Parliament and in the freedom and independence of the citizen which I have outlined in this chapter in the light of my career in the Westminster-Whitehall network. Lord Hailsham, with the authority of a Lord Chancellor, has made the most dramatic proposals. These include: A written constitution to define and limit the powers of Government, a Bill of Rights to entrench individual freedoms, a federal House of Commons, an elected House of Lords, and wider use of referenda to decide major issues.

A written constitution, if it ever came to pass, could consolidate America's First Amendment to guarantee the freedom and independence of the media. Other campaigners demand a Freedom of Information Act which would reinforce the powers of investigation and scrutiny, and incorporate at the same time the experience of the United States and Sweden. All very idealistic, with an overwhelming case in favour of each. But they all share this massive handicap: they can only become effective by legislation, and all my experience confirms that there is not in the foreseeable future the slightest chance of them ever being introduced and enacted. The ardour of Oppositions for reforms to curb Governments and herald a more open democratic system in Whitehall cools automatically when they take office. Even such a good Tory radical as Lord Hailsham, who has been a leading minister in several Conservative Governments, only made his most ambitious proposals for reform when he reached the elder statesman's rôle—in opposition. All-party agreement would be the answer, of course, but it is a distant dream.

Instead of waiting for many more decades—in the remote hope that someone some day will introduce the reforms identified above as urgent and desirable which cannot (in the words of the Lords Reform preamble proposal of 1911) brook any further delay—far better to make significant progress over a wide front simultaneously. This is the only formula likely to restore some of the old sovereignty of Parliament which has been stolen by the Executive and is now locked away in the vaults of Whitehall, ruled by its secret society of mandarins.

It is possible to introduce all the reforms mentioned in this chapter by administrative action, given the will in the Executive and the combined determination of Parliament, Press and People. They include: (i) A network of more powerful Select Committees on the Washington model to re-assert the old authority of Parliament over Ministers and civil servants, (ii) more independence and a higher calibre of MPs, (iii) more consultation and openness in a free society, (iv) more access to information and background facts about policies before they become enacted, (v) lowering of secrecy and administrative barriers against the media's investigative priorities and practices. Many bitter battles have still to be fought and won, for the lessons of one man's lifetime are clear and emphatic: the Executive will not voluntarily surrender an inch of the occupied territory which has been acquired and filched with such subtlety and calculation as essential to the elective dictatorship and the non-elective despotism.

6

THE PROBLEMS ARE
ALWAYS THE SAME

If we exclude the demands of Empire, which occupied so much time of the Parliaments and Governments of the inter-war years, the unending world crisis created by the dictators and the inevitability of war, one impression overshadows all others: the problems which preoccupied Ministers and MPs in the thirties are identical to those which confront the present generation of Ministers and members. When the author decided it was time to go he felt he had solved the mysteries of time and had reached the point when he had first entered the cloisters. Not only were Ministers debating the seemingly same problems and policies he first reported nearly fifty years ago but he was convinced that the two front benches were speaking from draft briefs and 'replies-to-questions' which first did duty a working life-time before!

The modern debates about unemployment, the need to protect basic national and local industries from cheap foreign competition, the dangers from abroad facing the farming and fishing industries; housing, health and education, import quotas, and so on, were the instant replays of very old records. The cynic might claim that this proves that Parliament never settles anything permanently, that it is of the essence of democracy that compromise decides only for the short-term and never for good. At least a reporter's old notebooks confirm that the old headaches and crises never go away. Every succeeding generation of politicians inherit the insolubles from their predecessors and dutifully bequeath them to their successors.

STATE AID TO LAME DUCKS
At the present time controversies recur daily about the state of the nation's public and private industries and the evils or merits of State intervention in private firms and industries, like British Leyland, Rolls Royce, Upper Clyde Shipbuilders and countless others. In my early years intervention was holy writ, and the Conservatives were the great wor-

shippers and believers in the sanctity of State aid to private industries, with no nonsense about unsightly lame ducks being unclean. Here are some examples from my case-book of the period. Subsidies and protective tariffs to keep the iron and steel industries on their feet; State aid to speed and encourage the reorganisation and modernisation of the Lancashire cotton industry weakened by cheap foreign imports; subsidies to the merchant and tramp shipping industries; massive State aid to shipbuilders; hefty grants to keep the mine-owners and railway companies solvent; grants to London's transport companies to keep the wheels turning; subsidies to the herring industry.

It was the age when Parliament, parties, Government, Whitehall and the great basic industries were groping towards the first formula for a mixed economy. In response to Labour's protests that the Conservatives were distributing State largesse to bolster private firms and industries and support City shares of bankrupt industries—how well old phrases have stood the test of time—the National (Conservative-dominated) Government of the thirties established an entirely new battery of State-appointed Boards, Corporations and Councils to ensure that the public money went for the urgent needs prescribed by Whitehall. Today's National Enterprise Board is a pale pink imitation of those true-blue pioneers.

Nowhere was this remarkable enterprise more fertile in producing hybrids between private enterprise and State direction than in agriculture. The Minister of Agriculture of the day, Walter Elliot, was one of the best political brains produced by the Scottish Unionists. Appropriate in one who had been a Labour leader in his student days at Glasgow University, he was non-doctrinaire in assessing the future of free enterprise. So he proceeded to introduce and launch on the farming industry an endless succession of Marketing Boards of all sorts and sizes to provide help and leadership to British farmers to modernise themselves. Marketing Boards were established for milk, pigs, beef, sugar beet, cheese, and other basic foods, with subsidies to assist the manufacture of cheese and butter. Walter Elliot was a man of remarkable ingenuity. He devised the milk-in-schools scheme. It was an astonishing breakthrough, marrying the State and private enterprise in idealistic harmony; on the one hand showing generous charity in satisfying the nutritional needs of the deprived youngsters in the years of the great depression while at the same time using State funds to bring profitability to milk production and hard-pressed dairy farmers and cheese-pressers. This captured the spirit of the age, to impart a social conscience to State intervention in private industries and firms. It is still being pursued as the seventies close and the eighties open.

Overshadowing all social and economic policies then, as now, was mass unemployment. Shortly before I moved in at Westminster the workless total touched the three million mark. As I leave the scene there seems a real possibility, despite frequent fluctuations, of the unemployment total breaking the two million barrier as the eighties arrive. But one must record with relief this distinction between then and now: the contemporary social service benefits have removed the most degrading features of hardship, poverty, hunger, malnutrition, and the abuse of human and family dignity. This is one sector where social justice has moved on, and where the welfare state has transformed the plight of the most depressed groups in our society, relieving the hardship of those dogged by misfortune.

THE TERRIBLE THIRTIES

There have been attempts recently to rehabilitate the depressed twenties and thirties, to dress and powder the record in order to show that it was not such a bad period after all. Some sociologists who were born in the post-war years and grew to maturity in the 'never-had-it-so-good' sixties—when too much affluence seemed to pose the greatest socio-economic problems imaginable—have tried to soften the harshness of the slump. Graphs and tables have been compiled in order to prove that the thirties were painted blacker than they really were and that the three million unemployed had much to be grateful for. What a travesty of reality! Those who lived through the terrible years are under no illusions, although there may have been a percentage of young men who were unaffected by the economic and social deprivation of the era, and were able to interpret history in later life from a privileged viewpoint.

But the attempts to soft-sell the 1930s as the not-so-terrible-years-after-all, coloured by the hindsight of the Oxbridge glow of the period or from the second-hand studies by young researchers born long after the war, simply will not wash. Having experienced the conditions then and now, one can only add the personal judgment that the naked gut hardship of the thirties was of a primitive cruelty and humiliation which is impossible for the post-Beveridge generations to imagine and for the young historians to feel, because their only conception of what the slump and depression really was like is written about from the comparative comfort of a subsequent generation—but never experienced at first hand. Those whose noses were rubbed in the depression share a more realistic version of history, not at all softened by memory. One thing is certain: the dumb acceptance of hunger and hardship in the 1930s will not be the hallmark of deprived people should stark depression on that scale ever come again.

Let the old Parliamentary records speak for themselves. Among the

92

author's early experiences of life at Westminster was the Unemployment Bill to cope with the misery of Poor Law relief and the humiliation of the soup kitchen. Then the higher refinements of official jargon sought to distinguish between derelict, depressed and distressed areas, with more fine distinctions drawn between those who were genuinely seeking work and those who had been unemployed for so long that they could never work again, fit only for the disused scrapheaps reserved for rejected humanity. The Government of the day resisted strong demands to increase the allowance for each dependent child from 2s. to 3s. per week (from 10p to 15p in modern currency) and to remove the precondition, inspired by a bureaucratic draftsman far removed from the distressed areas, that an unemployed father had to prove that he was 'unable to find suitable employment' before family relief would be permissible. The wording was said at the time to be an improvement on the original wording requiring an unemployed applicant to prove that he had not 'failed to avail himself of any opportunity for suitable employment'. This was the time when Harold Macmillan's 'Stockton conscience' first started gripping the young progressive Tories into major revolt. It was only when the revolting Tories teamed up with the Labour and Liberal Oppositions that concessions were wrung from the Government in assessing family needs. The National Register for 1934 solemnly recorded for posterity that 'by this show of generosity the Bill was later given a smooth passage'.

So my pencil and notebook are put away for good with a sense of relief that the modern State administering the social services has a more humane public face. At least my successors will not have to perform delicate verbal distinctions, as I did, between 'able-bodied relief', 'Poor Law relief', and 'Public Assistance', a task not made any easier when half a million human beings were described in hard-core terms in a Bill 'for whom there seems not the slightest prospects of employment in the future' while another 1,500,000 were so destitute that they had to go to local councils to seek Poor Law relief. Debates and votes of censure were frequent about closure of pits, the plight of 'blighted areas', and special commissioners to deal with the worst hit areas of depression.

Another flashback is relevant. The case made earlier in this book that MPs asserted more independence from party Whips than their successors of today is confirmed by the revolt mentioned above of a group of young Tories on the poverty issue which affected millions of workless families. The Government proposed that the precondition for getting relief was that the unemployed man had to show that he had been 'genuinely seeking work'. Thanks to Harold Macmillan and his fellow rebels—they were derided then by the tougher muscled colleagues as the 'Young Men's Christian Association, YMCA'—the Government were defeated by close

93

on a hundred majority. Similar revolts brought other crucial Government defeats and among further concessions won were that pensions for war wounds and maternity benefits would be disregarded in assessing relief.

These illustrations show the freedom and independence of back-bench MPs of all parties compared with the much greater discipline imposed by the party machines today. It was not a case that the party hierarchies were more tolerant of the liberal-minded Tories because they were the survivors of the lost generation massacred in the trenches. This independence was not confined to one type of MP. At the same time as the 'YMCA' idealists were aligning themselves with Labour and Liberal parties for more humane terms for the permanently unemployed, between seventy and eighty Right-wingers, broadly labelled as Right-wing Imperialists, Colonialists and military types, were trooping through the lobbies night after night for months on end voting against their Government's India Bill introducing the first major reforms which were to lead to independence. They were never disciplined either. The parties showed greater tolerance of revolts and permissiveness than is conceivable today under the greater centralised rigidity built into the new party bureaucracies.

YOUNG GEORGE BROWN

There was then, too, a generous recognition that each party was a coalition within itself, very much on the lines of the Republican and Democratic Parties in the United States. This was true not only of the Conservative Party, as the examples quoted above illustrate. The Labour Party also was much more permissive.

I recall one example, highly relevant to the Labour Party of today, that the Left-wingers formed their own Socialist League and actually held their own two-day conference at Leeds on May 20 and 21, 1938, under Sir Stafford Cripps. It is true that a little later Cripps, Aneurin Bevan and George Strauss were expelled from the party, but not for the crime of running the Socialist League as a rival body but for their defiance of official policy in creating a Popular Front with the Communists, Liberals and some deviationist Tories—similar to the more successful Popular Front Government in France. The motion for their expulsion was moved, as I remember, by a brilliant young boy orator from the constituencies named George Brown, who stirred the annual conference by his demands for loyalty and the eternal damnation of infidels who defied the faith. Cripps and Bevan survived the ordeal to become canonised in Labour's hallowed memories, Strauss to become the 'Father of the House of Commons'—and George Brown to expel himself forty years later for the party's failure to keep up with his interpretation of the holy writ. At the same time as Cripps, Bevan and Strauss were the rebel martyrs, Harold

94

Macmillan, on the Tory side, opted for the wilderness, too, in protest against his party's leaders, whom he derided as extinct volcanoes and disused slag-heaps. Rebels of those days still had the reasonable prospect of being honoured and even reaching the highest offices in the land, including Premiership. Could one contemplate the post-war Bevanites or today's Tribune Group, the equivalents of the old Socialist League, getting away with their own two-day conference to rival and challenge Labour's official annual confessional? Or of any of today's leading Conservatives of the eminence of Winston Churchill or Harold Macmillan enthusiastically joining bodies hostile to the official leadership—Churchill with his India League and Macmillan on the platform launching Lloyd George's 'Council for Action'—and then rejoining the party on their own terms and ending up at No. 10 Downing Street?

One of the most striking features of my first and last notebooks from Westminster (separated by close on a half-century) includes two identical issues, admittedly each with new features and aspects but basically posing the very same problems. The bitter controversies over the past year or so, first over Iceland expelling British trawlers from her waters and then Britain trying to exclude the Common Market countries from UK waters extended fifty miles and beyond, are merely the other side of an old record. In 1934 I solemnly reported, in the first prorogation speech I heard, the Government's proud claim that a measure had been successfully placed on the statute book suppressing illegal trawling by foreign ships and providing for hefty fines and long prison sentences for skippers. Then, of course, the routine patrol fishery vessels could always whistle up ships of the Royal Navy, then in abundance and always available on the high seas, to reinforce the patrols if any skipper proved unco-operative when required to be escorted to UK ports. Inshore fishermen and the near water herring boats were provided with similar protection. Last year, when Icelandic gunboats were accused in the British papers of acts of piracy when they tried to cut the nets of our long-distance trawlers fishing off *their* home waters, the only difference was that in the interval we had slipped back significantly in the naval league.

One is struck not by the vast changes which have been effected in the Parliamentary scene but rather by what has remained unchanged. Even the industries which claimed the headlines half-a-century ago are the same, which suggests that the more Parliament and Government fuss over particular problems the more persistent and intransigent the problems become: coal, closure of pits, railways, shipping, shipbuilding, typewriters, cars, cotton textiles, woollens, cheap imports from abroad, our declining native industries.

After half-a-century one becomes word perfect. Today's tensions between London and Dublin over Ulster and a united Ireland? Not a word, not a comma, has been changed in the script. Forty-five years ago I solemnly reported J. H. Thomas, Dominions Secretary, announcing in the Commons: 'We are ready at any time to enter into negotiations with the Irish Free State Government for the settlement of all outstanding questions if a satisfactory basis for discussion can be found.' The search goes on through blood and tears. Scottish Nationalists and Devolution? The official Labour Opposition in 1934 demanded a Royal Commission not to consider but 'to prepare for Home Rule for Scotland'. The Government replied that the time was not quite ready. Home Rule was then official Labour policy and the word devolution had not been coined. Many last laments have been played on the pipes since then.

NORTH SEA SCROLLS

North Sea oil? It is probably the oddest story of all. In March 1934 Parliament passed a Bill setting up conditions for prospecting for oil and providing: 'That the ownership of all oil that might be found should be vested in the State, so that there would be no private royalties.' It now seems an alien revolutionary idea from an overwhelming Conservative Government and Parliament compared with today's attitudes. In fact, Tory Ministers enthusiastically commended the oil enterprise. In particular, the highest priest of all, the Marquis of Londonderry, announced in the House of Lords on 19 April, 1934, that as a strong upholder of the rights of private property he had been 'much exercised over the proposal in the Bill to nationalise oil deposits but I have come to the conclusion that this is the only way in which to secure their exploitation on proper lines'. For good measure this champion of high Toryism added that the principle was not all that new anyway, as the State already 'claimed all gold and silver found in the country and all coal mined under the sea'. Under the sea, forsooth. The Conservative Party leaders shrugged off the protests from their Right-wingers that they were going in for 'confiscation'. Whether the Conservative Party has advanced or retreated, during the intervening years, on State ownership and State spending in prospecting for and profits from oil wells is a good point for study by the keepers of the party's North Sea scrolls.

The House of Lords, too, provides another striking example of the permanence of unsolved problems. The more agitated both major parties have become about the need for reform the more the old House remains the same, resistant to any radical change. At the moment both the Tory and Labour Parties are pledged to major reform. The Tories have a masterplan for a new second chamber with a constitution of hereditary, nominated and elected peers. The plan is so drastic that it amounts to the effective abolition of the chamber, however the current reforming Tory leaders trim the ermine. And the Labour Party is pledged to wipe out the Lords and create a second chamber which would be subordinate to the Commons, shorn of all its old powers. Here, too, the parties have been panting to keep up with history at a standstill. At my first Labour conference, on 1 October, 1934, at Southport, the party was starry-eyed over its resolution to wipe out the Lords as a legislative assembly as one of the first acts of a future Labour Government. The phrase wafts gently over the years: abolition was essential to destroy any threat of 'sabotage by the Lords'. As for the very newest ideas from Mrs Thatcher, the Earl of Home, Lord Carrington and others, for a new chamber, they are really fifty years behind their party. Neville Chamberlain, when he was Conservative Party overlord running the Central Office as Prime Minister-in-waiting in the very early thirties, produced his blueprint to have a new House of Lords drawn equally from hereditary and nominated groups, two hundred strong. His plan is to be found among his private papers in the university archives of his native Birmingham. He was probably more detached than other reformers. At the end of his Premiership he was offered an earldom. He declined it. 'I want to die plain Mr Chamberlain, just like my father.'

The fact is that nobody gets excited over Lords reform any more. It is nearly seventy years since the Asquith Government declared that it brooked no delay. My own view is that newspapermen will still be scribbling away thirty and fifty years hence on the future of their Lordships' House.

A CENTRE PARTY?

It is the same story with the hardy annual of political realignment of the Centre, in order to get rid of the difficult customers like Tory diehards and Labour militant rebels of the Left. The great personalities of the First World War and the early twenties also wanted to form a Centre Party. One of my first exercises in writing about politics was concerned with a clarion call in the early thirties by over a hundred MPs to drop the sectional labels like Conservative, Liberal and Labour and rally round a great National Party. Even Neville Chamberlain, Prime Minister designate at the time, saw it as a splendid opportunity to get rid of that 'obnoxious term of Conservative'. Forty years on, the dream of a new party formed from Labour's Social Democrats, the Liberals and the pro gressive Conservatives in the tradition of R. A. Butler, Iain Macleod and Edward Boyle encourages more happy day dreams. Nothing, however, ever happens towards reconstruction. The Labour and Conservative Parties remain the same, yesterday, today and tomorrow, each a coalition of ever-moving forces within itself. And as for electoral reform, now an 'urgent' issue, it was even more urgent and imminent fifty years ago, when a Bill for PR and the alternative vote was actually given a second reading when introduced by MacDonald's Labour Government with Liberal blessing. But the onset of the National Government in 1931 kyboshed the plan. Now two generations later the current politicos are panting to catch up where their grandfathers left off.*

* Inflation was largely unknown as a word in the twenties and thirties, whereas it dominates all human life today. Perhaps Neville Chamberlain, when he was Chancellor of the Exchequer, discovered the secret which has eluded all his successors. This was how the editor of the *National Register*, erecting his signposts to guide future historians and researchers, described the miracle: 'For the first time in years wages in 1934 showed a tendency to rise, and as the cost of living did not increase the rise in the standard of living was real as well as nominal, enabling a partial restoration of the cuts in pay and services imposed three years earlier.' That was the last time in history that wages, prices, public and private spending came up with the right mix. I was there to record for posterity the one notable achievement which has never been repeated and which my successors are unlikely to experience!

7

THE DEVIL'S DECADE

There were many other notable characteristics of Britain in the nine-teen-thirties besides the glamour and colour of Imperial power. It was also the decade of the dictatorships and the crises and cruelties they begat by which it is possible to compare our stature and role then and now. The period was unique by the extent to which mass waves of public anger, emotion and protest, combined with a highly articulate and orchestrated public opinion, dominated politics and influenced Governments, Parliaments and the media to a degree we are unlikely to see reproduced even in today's conditions when the sophisticated techniques of communications make it easier for the public's responses to be reported and manipulated for the national screen. It was the last occasion when the force and intensity of mass opinion not merely made a powerful impact on Britain's policies at home and abroad, but also when Governments were influenced, conditioned and even actively intimidated and pressured by mass thinking and protest on a nation-wide scale. I have seen nothing remotely like this highly charged inter-action between Government and governed in the forty years which followed. There lies one of the secrets to an understanding of the MacDonald-Baldwin-Chamberlain era, for what has become known as The Devil's Decade will continue to fascinate and stimulate future generations of students and scholars long after the sixties and seventies are forgotten.

It has been the vogue in recent years to theorise about the ideals of participation in decision-sharing at the centre. It was practised spontaneously on a mass scale in the thirties. Reporting the constant crises of the period, I can testify that this reached a peak during the Spanish Civil War when the intensity of emotional anger and protest possessed the entire nation to a degree that was never totally recaptured during the subsequent convulsions over Hitler and Mussolini. The explanation can be briefly narrated from personal experience, not from the twenty-twenty vision of hindsight formed after poring over official Cabinet papers.

When it was realised that Hitler, Mussolini and Stalin were exploiting the cruelties perpetrated on the Spanish people because of the dictators' ambitions, not least by the Luftwaffe's bombing of defenceless towns, the British people were gripped by a tempestuous sense of outrage. The reaction was most significant. For the first time in history all artists, writers, musicians, students in the mass, teachers and members of all professions formed a mighty army of public opinion. It was a spontaneous eruption. It was the highest peak of articulate passion ever to possess the nation's intellectuals and educated classes, not as the product of a highly organised manipulation of emotions and minds but as a genuine uprising in angry protest. This was the first time that these essentially middle class groups and the army of students had come together with the mass movements of the Left in a national rising formed for a common cause. In social and political terms this marked a major breakthrough in realignment of class and social loyalties and identities, for here were the new young generation of young men from public schools, universities and middle-class homes eager to link arms in a shared idealism with the working classes.

The scale and intensity of this evolution proved overwhelming, the more so when one recalls that the same forces from the identical class and social backgrounds had eagerly co-operated solidly against the workers in the General Strike of 1926 in order to smash trade union solidarity. In the mid-thirties volunteers enrolled enthusiastically to fight in Spain against the dictators. Artists' and writers' companies were formed; an Attlee Brigade of what would be regarded to-day as 'freedom fighters' was formed in honour of Labour's leader and future Prime Minister. But even if the volunteers for the front line failed to save the Republican Government from defeat, the movement at home produced two shattering political upheavals which helps to explain much of the mystery of the thirties: the Left Book Club and the Peace Pledge Union.

LEFT BOOK CLUB
Victor Gollancz's Left Book Club was formed to organise and give voice to the forces of the Left. Yellow-jacketed books cascaded in thousands every week on an eager consuming public demanding more of the highly polemical, controversial and aggressive propaganda. Each book was guaranteed an enormous sale which makes today's publishers' normal prints appear puny by comparison. This publishing enterprise had a profound effect in not merely articulating the Left's idealism but also in providing a hard cutting edge of angry protest to political propaganda. It went so far Left in its activist pro-Communist propaganda that Herbert Morrison demanded that the Left Book Club be proscribed because it was attempting, he claimed, to capture the constituency parties for Com-

munist sympathisers and split the Labour Party—the identical indictment which this newsman had to report in the same words against the Bevanites and the Tribunites thirty and forty years later, with Labour never changing its internal conflicts and the Left never advancing. Even so, the Left Book Club had the most powerful impact on the entire political thinking of the time and was a potent influence in producing the Attlee Government in 1945. In the middle and late thirties Gollancz sold millions of books to the Club's 50,000 subscribing members, and frequently overcrowded the Albert Hall with mass rallies—a remarkable publisher's achievement by any yardstick, especially when he could sell 220,000 copies of *Guilty Men*.

The rich flowering which reached its peak of power and influence over Spain faded very rapidly. The new forces which had come together in a popular front never seen before lost their idealism and momentum when they discovered that they were being exploited and manipulated by party activists, notably the Communists, anxious to harness the mass movement for party and propaganda ends. After Spain the non-political army of protest simply melted away in disillusionment and could not be reformed when the much greater atrocities and menace of Hitler and Mussolini were manifesting themselves. That is why the Spanish Civil War has a unique place in the history of the nineteen-thirties. Youthful idealism was finally destroyed by the Hitler-Stalin pact of August 1939.

One of the greatest paradoxes of the thirties was that despite the surfeit of *revolutionary* issues and campaigns in an age of violence, aggravated by the mass hardship of nearly three million unemployed, the country never swung to Communism or any other political and social extremism. Even in 1922, Walter Newbold, who won Motherwell as a Communist, wired Lenin: 'Glasgow won for Communists.' He was referring to the fact that 'Red Clydeside' had won ten out of the fifteen Glasgow seats for the Independent Labour Party. Revolution was in the air, but not Communism. The Left-wing ILP, the biggest force in the Labour movement of the time, occupied broadly the far Left stance of the latter-day Bevanites and Tribunites, but with this distinction: the ILP were always vigorously anti-Communist and this explains why Communism made so little progress in the inter-war years when so many events and pressures were going that way—and why indeed the Communists failed to make any major breakthrough in 'Red Clydeside'. This is the key to the political understanding of the thirties: that however revolutionary the mood was in idealistic terms it never embraced extremism. Even halfway through the decade, with no relief in sight to the staggering unemployment figures, the people returned the Baldwin Government with a thumping majority at the 1935 election.

But any detached study of the forces which swept politics and the Parliament of the period must concede the highest recognition to the famous Peace Pledge Union Ballot, which had a profounder impact and influence on Government policy than any other civil non-political eruption of popular opinion in history. Lord Cecil, the great champion of the League of Nations, organised the popular referendum with the support of Labour, Liberal and a substantial part of the Left-progressive Tories under Harold Macmillan. All the papers at the time forecast that the campaign would be a mighty flop and finally expose and humiliate the mass of idealists of the period, the more so as the saintly Lord Cecil was derided as having his heart in the Middle Ages and his head in the clouds. Close on twelve million people voted in 1935: 90 per cent were for the League of Nations, disarmament, peace, collective security; 80 per cent for the abolition of air forces; 90 per cent in favour of economic sanctions against Italy because of Mussolini's invasion of Abyssinia, with 74 per cent in favour of military sanctions.

When these figures were announced at a mass rally at the Albert Hall in April 1935, presided over by the Archbishop of Canterbury, to demonstrate the ballot's Christian morality and non-party idealism, the impact was shattering. Whatever the fine shadings in meaning, the overall impression was powerfully created that the country was for peace and pacifism while at the same time declaring military support, with hand on heart, for all measures to stop Hitler and Mussolini provided that they did not land us in war. It proved the classic example of a national state of schizophrenia, as more than 80 per cent voted against aggression and an equal number—the same people answering the different question—against arms and any idea of rearmament. In effect, it was a referendum for peace carrying great political influence.

As a newsman of the period, I remain convinced that the Peace Ballot had a more powerful effect in influencing the history of the thirties—the failure to halt the dictators, thus making the outbreak of war inevitable—than any other single factor. When Stanley Baldwin was presented with the figures by Archbishop Lang he blandly claimed that the figures proved the power of the 'large body of opinion behind us in the efforts we are making to maintain the authority of the League of Nations. We value this support.' But it cracked the nerve of the National Government, coming so soon after the famous East Fulham by-election where a massive Tory majority in a Tory stronghold was converted into an equally massive Labour majority. This could only be interpreted by the Government as a pacific country voting for pacifism.

If Winston Churchill had fought a by-election anywhere in the country on a programme for rearmament and standing up to the dictators whatever the cost he would have been overwhelmingly defeated. Women exerted the most powerful influence of all in dictating the political mood of the nation forty years before the high tide of Women's Lib in the seventies. They had lost husbands, fathers and sons in the First World War which had ended only sixteen years before. Most Conservatives, who formed the massive majority enjoyed by the National Government, became overawed by the pacifist flood sweeping the country.

Historians searching for a clue to the contradictions of the thirties should start with the Peace Pledge Union Ballot and the Fulham by-election. Together these pacifist demonstrations decided the policies of the period. Without doubt they delayed rearmament and frustrated and still more isolated Winston Churchill. The nation did not want to be roused by anyone; the miracle was that rearmament let alone conscription ever got off the ground. The Premiers of the time—MacDonald, Baldwin, Chamberlain—did not defy or betray the British people in the Devil's Decade: they personified and expressed the mood; they were the products of their age.

Where the Governments of the thirties showed much greater courage was in conquering the challenges to law and order at home coming alike from the Fascists and to a lesser extent the Communists. At least on this issue Ramsay MacDonald, Stanley Baldwin and Neville Chamberlain got their priorities right and rescued the country from the danger of civil war and communal bloodshed. It was by far the ugliest and most terrifying experience in my time as a journalist. It was even more dangerous to the nation's unity than war itself. By comparison, the rowdy demonstrations by the National Front and its clashes with the Left-wing International Socialists and Trotskyists of recent years are peevish diversions.

Led by Sir Oswald Mosley, a former Labour MP, the Fascist movement—there were a few rival groupings—came dangerously close to becoming a popular mass movement, bidding for power by slavishly copying identical methods of para-military processions, challenge and violence to those which carried Hitler and Mussolini to power.

THE FASCIST THREAT

I have never seen, even in war-time, anything comparable to the primitive intolerance and strong-arm brutality I witnessed in the marches through the East End of London on Sunday afternoons. Some seven thousand Blackshirts, imitating the Fascist and Nazi methods in Rome, Munich and Berlin, used to march through the Jewish areas of the East End in the most provocative display of quasi-militarism and might and discipline. Counter-demonstrations were staged by the Communists and other Left-wing groups. The Jewish communities showed great self-control, courage, and dignity. The Fascists were closer to becoming a mass movement than they ever imagined, but for one classic blunder: on 7 June, 1934, they held what they intended to be their most commanding display of influence and mass popular appeal. Unfortunately for them, they allowed it to be seen as a demonstration of physical brutality and cruelty. I recall there were many influential Tory MPs in front row seats that night to see for themselves the delirium and ecstasy of Fascism in action. If the Fascist leaders had only been able to restrain their militant followers they were nearer to the point of a breakdown in law and order than is possible for researchers four decades later to recapture from old reports. In a well-drilled exercise of might, the Blackshirts were merciless in bashing and physically beating and manhandling counter-demonstrators. Those scenes, as I saw them, finally scared and terrified the great mass of people sympathetic to the need to rescue the country from the menace of Communism and the danger of a Kremlin-style dictatorship in Whitehall. One night of terror and violence was sufficient. The spectre of blood, rioting and civil war shocked the Government. With unusual speed a law was rushed through prohibiting the wearing of uniforms.

As an observer of the turbulent scenes, the frightening and provocative marches with military-style discipline, and then the display of violent brutality at the mass rally at Olympia, originally designed as a showpiece to impress the Establishment, I am in no doubt about how close Britain came to civil conflict on a mass scale. It was during the depths of the Depression and conditions were ripe for extremism, the more so as the Fascist and Nazi solutions for unemployment and the Communist new order in Russia evoked much sympathy and hope throughout Britain. The Blackshirts were in fact making very much bigger inroads into the Conservatives' far Right than the Communists were in Labour's far Left. If more restraint had been imposed at Olympia by the Blackshirt stewards in dealing with interrupters the Fascists would have developed as a powerful political force in the country. But the public exhibition of primitive violence by thugs finally convinced the Right-wing Tories and sympathisers of the terrifying consequences of importing the Nazi and Fascist methods into Britain.

To the credit of the Parliament of the thirties, the political parties did not seek panic remedies to cope with the challenge to law and order. After the prohibition of uniforms the entire Fascist movement, deprived of its common but anonymous identity, lost its sparkle and appeal, and spluttered to extinction. It was a mighty deliverance from catastrophe. Until September 1939. . . .

8

CHURCHILL: THE MYTH AND THE FACTS

One of the most persistent and treasured myths of our time is that in the thirties Winston Churchill was the leader of a mass national movement, clamouring to overthrow Neville Chamberlain's appeasement policy and to stop Hitler before his Panzer divisions and Luftwaffe squadrons could destroy Europe. And that Churchill was prevented from rescuing Britain and the world from the holocaust to come by a group of old men like Neville Chamberlain, Stanley Baldwin, Ramsay MacDonald, and John Simon. This is complete historical fantasy; it may help to salve a nation's guilty conscience but it has no relation to reality. Conservative, Labour and Liberal apologists cherish the illusion that Winston was really their folk hero at the time and that their champion would have triumphed over evil if only the guilty men of Munich had not so thwarted popular will. Recalling my daily reporting of contemporary history as it was actually happening and not trying to reconstruct and rationalise it from hindsight, I cannot support the legend since accepted by popular history. In this zeal for escapism, the search for alibis, a totally false picture of pre-war Churchill has been created. For one of the greatest ironies of all time is that it was really Hitler who rescued Churchill for Britain, the free world and history.

NOBODY'S HERO

Throughout the thirties—The Devil's Decade—Winston Churchill was hero to nobody. He had no following, no meaningful group, no supporters. At Westminster his loyalists could be counted on the fingers of one hand. Nobody wanted to know him. He was untouchable. Throughout those crises-racked years he was the loneliest figure I have seen in public life. He was despised, avoided, mistrusted. He was politically ostracised, regarded as dangerous, unreliable and erratic. He was seen as a failed politician, a man with a past but no future: 'a busted flush' as Lord Beaverbrook described him.

Indeed, if Adolf Hitler, for once, had only decided to stop shouting about 'My patience is exhausted' and schemed instead to lay his plans for European conquest on a longer-term basis he might have found himself even more powerful and invincible in 1940 after he had over-run Western Europe and Britain stood alone, bracing herself for invasion. Because then Winston Churchill would not have become the great war-time Prime Minister, to inspire the desperate defiance of the British people when all seemed lost. For he would not have been in Parliament.

In the spring and summer of 1939, when Hitler was planning to invade Poland after having seized Czechoslovakia and Austria for the Third Reich, in London plans were being prepared to ditch Churchill. He was seen in the ruling Conservative Party as such a squalid nuisance—a dangerous warmonger defying Chamberlain's appeasement policies— that secret discussions were going ahead to disown him as Tory member and candidate in his Epping constituency and to replace him by a true-blue party loyalist. According to electoral law governing Britain's quin-quennial system, the Parliament elected on 14 November, 1935, would have ended its maximum life in November 1940. Thus the general election would normally have taken place at the very latest in the spring or early summer of 1940. If only Herr von Ribbentrop, the German Foreign Minister and former Ambassador to Great Britain, had advised Hitler about such constitutional refinements of the British democratic system, and of the mounting pressures among the top Tories to dump Churchill, the invasion of Poland might have been postponed by some six months to see whether Churchill would be defeated in Epping. Of this there can be no doubt. The pacific mood in the country would have made Churchill's ousting and ultimate defeat at the polls certain. Then there would have been no Churchill available to personify and inspire Britain's survival when the whole of Western Europe was under Nazi and Fascist rule. Without Churchill could Britain have survived alone? Those of us report-ing the day-by-day events of those years were in no doubt: Britain without Churchill would have been in the mood to seek peace on the most honour-able terms negotiable.

This is not a fanciful reconstruction of history. Winston Churchill throughout the nineteen-thirties stood alone. In the Conservative Party he was seen as a traitor. Twice he had betrayed and left them. They had long memories and could not forget how he had lashed them with his searing eloquence for over three decades. Technically he was a Conservative in the thirties, but he was not of them or with them. And any idea that the people were prepared to vote for his rearmament policies to stop Hitler was grotesque. He scared everybody. The Conservative indictment against him was formidable; he had a long record of continuous and unrelieved rebellion against their successive leaders, whom he sought to destroy. They could never forgive him. So the central organisation, and the Whips in the Commons in particular, were planning to get rid of him for good. The paradox of history is that Hitler, by invading Poland when he did, saved Churchill from these Conservatives' hopes to wreak vengeance upon him for his disloyalty. Hitler, by his miscalculation, by rushing the invasion of Poland, helped to guarantee that the greatest warrior-statesman of all was available at Westminster to ensure the German dictator's final humiliation in his Berlin bunker on 30 April, 1945, and the surrender of the German forces on Lüneburg Heath on 7 May, 1945, to Field-Marshal Montgomery. Without Churchill, Hitler's Third Reich might well have survived if not for the thousand years he promised at least very much longer than 1945.

To appreciate the feelings which gripped the overwhelming mass of Conservatives in Government, at Westminster and in the country towards Churchill throughout the thirties it is essential to understand the intensity of anger which his very name aroused, because of his 'crime sheet' and his earlier desertions to the enemy. They never forgave him for 'betraying his class' when he joined the great Liberal Government of 1905. The wounds in secret never healed, they festered for thirty years. Most of all they could never forget his lacerating tongue. For instance: 'We know perfectly well what to expect—a party of great vested interests, banded together in a formidable federation: corruption at home, aggression abroad to cover it up . . . . sentiment by the bucketful, patriotism by the imperial pint; the open hand at the public exchequer, the open door at the public house; dear food for the millions, cheap labour for the millionaire.' The wounds suppurated. Ten years later the Conservative leader of the time, and later Prime Minister, Bonar Law, agreed to join the war-time coalition with Lloyd George in 1916 only on condition that Churchill was excluded from high office. If Law had not died in 1922 Churchill would never have been brought back to join the Conservative 1924–29 Government as Chancellor under Stanley Baldwin.

'CRIMES' AGAINST ESTABLISHMENT
From 1930 onwards, especially after resigning from the Tories' Shadow Cabinet in January 1931, he was in continuous state of open rebellion against the party. For the whole of the thirties he sought, on a series of major issues, to destroy successive Tory Governments, overthrow their leaders, and split the party. They could never forgive his ridicule. A generation after the vituperation about the Tories' 'imperial pint patriotism'

he was back on the old routine with this picture of the Conservative Governments of the thirties: '. . . Decided only to be undecided, resolved to be irresolute, adamant for drift . . . solid for fluidity, all powerful for impotence.' The spoken word doesn't come better than that any more!

On every important issue of the pre-war decade Winston was in bitter conflict with the Conservative Establishment. In return they saw him as a political adventurer, a buccaneer without loyalities or moorings or friends, a dangerous character to be kept at arm's length. His magnetism and brilliance which later enraptured, repelled them then. But the truth remains that the Conservatives bitterly disliked and distrusted him; he was ready to desert the Tory and Liberal Parties with impunity whenever it suited his book.

It is not necessary to go over the first twenty odd years of the century to catalogue Churchill's 'crimes' against Conservative doctrine, and why, in 1939, plans were far advanced to expel him from the ranks. The thirties provided abundant offences to justify excommunication from the faith. He deliberately paraded his isolation after January 1931 when he resigned from the party's Shadow Cabinet in protest against Baldwin committing the party to constitutional reforms for India, the first step towards Dominion status and final independence. He was not to return to the party's inner counsels and become acceptable once more until September 1939. On the India Bill he became leader of the most powerful rebel group the Conservative Party has known this century. Throughout 1934–35 he led between seventy and eighty Right-wing MPs in nightly revolt against the Government. The size of this rebellion, sustained constantly week after week and month after month, makes subsequent revolts by the Tories Suez group over the canal and the Bevanite and Tribunite rebels in the Labour Party seem small-time affairs. He presided over the final convulsion of the old Imperialist Right-wing tradition in the Tory Party. Churchill had no time for Baldwin's liberalising ideas or the pressures for change in the sub-continent, which preceded by some twenty-five years Harold Macmillan's 'Wind of Change' in Africa. In Winston's eyes, the British Raj was permanent, with all its splendours, glories and romanticism he had seen in his young days. Gandhi he saw as a 'malignant and subversive fanatic, the naked fakir'. By temperament he could not understand the austerities of nakedness, fasting and non-resistance as the armour of power.

This was the period, too, when Winston impetuously committed his second unforgivable crime against the party's holy writ. He accused two of the most powerful and influential Conservative figures, Sir Samuel Hoare (then Secretary for India, later Foreign Secretary) and the Earl of Derby (head of one of the great territorial dynastic families who ruled the party) of tampering with evidence and witnesses from the Lancashire cotton industries to the Joint Select Committee on the India constitutional reforms. In the party of gentlemen such accusations were seen as an outrageous assault upon the integrity and character of two most honourable men. By this exercise he hoped at the same time to destroy and discredit Baldwin at the party conference. The Tory establishment wanted Churchill's scalp, for in their code of honour such conduct was intolerable. An all-party Committee of Privileges was set up to investigate Churchill's accusations. They unanimously reported against Churchill and dismissed his charges. He was further humiliated by a merciless exposure by Sir John Simon, Home Secretary, who used his great forensic skill to add to Winston's public disgrace. The report condemning his conduct was carried with 'acclamation' by Parliament. Not a voice was raised in his defence. He stood alone.

One of the oddest features of the whole India affair was the speed at which the seventy to eighty Right-wing Conservative MPs proceeded to drop Churchill immediately the India Bill was passed. In normal political alignments the group might have been expected to keep together, because of common interests, and re-form on Defence, Foreign, Imperial and Commonwealth issues. This never occurred with Churchill. He was dropped overnight. Once the Parliamentary fight over India was finished they deserted him and moved over at once to become loyal supporters first of Baldwin, then of Chamberlain. They never again hunted with Winston. This explains why he was such a lonely isolated figure when he developed his anti-appeasement policies. They did not want to be identified with him in opening up new anti-Government campaigns. The explanation was simple: they saw him as a born 'splitter'.

Nor did he attempt to work his passage or rescue himself from the widespread unpopularity which his efforts at the character assassination of Lord Derby and Sir Samual Hoare had aroused—he was never really forgiven for impugning the honour of these two 'Top Tories'—but proceeded to compound the magnitude of his offence. He carried his assault on the Tory leadership into the party's home base. Early in 1935 his son, Randolph, stood as the rebel independent Conservative candidate in the by-election at Wavertree, Liverpool. The son fought on the sire's policies; Winston enthusiastically supported Randolph, concentrating on the effects of the India reforms on the Lancashire cotton industry. Extreme penalties of expulsion were threatened against any Tory MPs who dared support the Churchill heretics. The Churchill challenge proved spectacularly successful. Randolph polled over 10,000 votes, coming within 3,000 of the official party candidate—thus presenting the safest of Tory seats to Labour. The Government's fury with the Churchills increased when overseas reactions exhibited a total lack of confidence in the Conservative Government. Foreigners, after Wavertree, saw Britain in a state of unrest, political chaos, and indiscipline. The apparent uncertainty and confusion in the ruling party led to a run on the pound and enormous amounts of funk money were withdrawn overnight, as Americans and others judged that Britain was cracking up and becoming ripe for extremism of every imaginable sort then rampant on the continent—Nazism, Fascism and Communism.

But Wavertree was not a singular spasm. Immediately after the 1935 general election the Churchills became involved in another anti-Government foray, this time into the Highland fortress of Ross and Cromarty. The two MacDonalds, father Ramsay and son Malcolm, lost their seats as National Labour Ministers and vacancies had to be found quickly for them if the Government was to retain its national character. So Malcolm MacDonald was duly adopted as National candidate supporting the Government for Ross and Cromarty (his father returned via the Scottish Universities), traditionally a safe Liberal seat. Randolph was nominated as independent Tory candidate by a breakaway group of the Unionist Association in the constituency; and the split was aggravated when the chairman, vice-chairman and other notables in the Tory Association resigned in protest against the Churchill invasion, especially as the son campaigned once again on his father's policies hostile to the Tory leadership. Direct action was taken to isolate the Churchills. Individual messages of support were sent to Malcolm MacDonald by the other party leaders in the National Government, notably by Stanley Baldwin and Sir John Simon. Randolph's revolt in the Highlands was described by Winston as 'unfortunate and inconvenient to me'. He did not wish the sins of the son to be visited on the father. At the time we political correspondents were writing on the prospects of Churchill being appointed Minister of Defence by Baldwin and he was full of hope. So he kept a low profile during the Ross and Cromarty campaign, and for a significant time his criticisms of the Government's defence policy and of Hitler were muted. He need not have worried. Winston was not invited to join the Government, due to Chamberlain's veto. Randolph failed ignominiously, saving his deposit by only 167 votes. This was in February 1936, five years after Winston split with the party leadership over India and much else—a long spell of disloyalty, continuous revolt and dissension in a party which he had previously left and rejoined with neither conviction nor enthusiasm. So the Churchill fortunes were at an all-time low. But much worse was to follow.

The most persistent criticism levelled against Winston Churchill was that he lacked judgment, and in the Abdication crisis he played into the hands of his critics by proving how abysmally he could get big issues distorted. He paid dearly and disastrously for his miscalculation and bad judgment. This was his greatest catastrophe. It convinced even his few friends and admirers that he had no stability, that he would always be an eccentric maverick. Even if every allowance is made for his generous motives—his romanticism, his personal loyalty to the young King, and his emotional response to the affairs of the heart—he emerged from the ordeal a tattered and discredited figure.

If the testimony of one's memory may be cited, I have never seen such concentrated fury and hatred directed from all sides of the Commons as that which Churchill experienced throughout the Abdication crisis. He was shocked and overwhelmed when he was howled down several times, especially when he persisted in raising questions and points of order after he had been ruled out of order. The anger he evoked came from all corners, but most of the bitterness directed against him came from the mass of Conservative MPs. His repudiation was merciless, his humiliation deep, the anger against him was overwhelming, as the pandemonium made it impossible for us in the Press Gallery to hear what he was trying to shout in defiance. On two days he was refused a hearing. I have never seen anyone so execrated and despised by colleagues in the same party. The mass of Conservatives wanted to excommunicate him for his disloyalty to the Government and party. Withdrawal of the Whip then would have finished him.

Baldwin kept his wilder colleagues in check. The Prime Minister could afford to be generous to the man who had tried for fifteen years to depose him. He showed magnanimity in victory. Baldwin, by his superb skills and judgment, had made himself the most popular man in the country —his speech, delivered spontaneously from scribbled headline cues on envelopes, was the greatest of many great speeches I have heard, masterly, moving, simple, low key, without any attempt at purple oratory. Churchill, in contrast, had made himself the most unpopular and discredited man in the country. It seemed inevitable that he had reached the end of the road with the Conservative Party. He knew that he had made the most calamitous of blunders. He feared that his career was finally in ruins: 'The unanimous view that my political life was at last ended,' he wrote in retrospect, when he paid tribute to Baldwin's 'shrewd judgment', in having 'perceived and expressed the profound will of the nation'. The price he was compelled to pay for his Abdication disaster was heavy and long. People who had been sympathetic to his warnings about the dangers inherent in Hitler's militarism at once deserted him after such crass misjudgment.

Robert Boothby (later Lord Boothby of Rattray Head) has captured the Churchill crisis of confidence in a sentence. He had been Parliamentary Private Secretary to the great man, and was one of the four members of Churchill's tiny group of disciples, and he felt impelled to write in protest that his few friends found it impossible to follow him because 'they cannot be sure where the hell they are going to be landed next'. Boothby has always asserted that Churchill had only four friends in the party throughout the thirties: son-in-law Duncan Sandys, devoted Brendan Bracken, Boothby himself, and General Sir Edward Spears. Nobody gave a higher estimate.

Thus Churchill's crimes against the Conservative Party and its leaders became more heinous. When Neville Chamberlain succeeded Stanley Baldwin as Prime Minister and party leader in 1937 Churchill simply transferred his attacks to the new man with mounting ferocity. In reaction to the incoming Premier's obsession with appeasement of the dictators Churchill's denunciation became ever more vehement and extreme, especially over the British Government's blindness to the mounting threats from Hitler's increasingly strident demands and ultimatums, accompanied by vast rearmament. He did this alone, without supporters. Contrary to the myth that has persisted since those days, Winston had no allies. As an observer of the scene and reporting the great events as they unfolded against a background of the most outrageous obscenities against human dignity, Churchill would be seen to be despised and rejected by everyone.

There was, of course, a great mass revulsion against appeasement of the German, Italian, Russian, Spanish and Japanese military dictatorships throughout the thirties. But this was very much Left-of-Centre, reflecting Labour, Liberal and Communist forces. This produced the ill-starred Popular Front, which reached its peak in 1936. It was the time of the famous Peace Pledge Union Ballot, when in 1935 nearly twelve million people signed for peace and the Conservatives lost a 'safe' seat at East Fulham by an astonishing swing in favour of pacifism, disarmament, and the ideal of peace and collective security. But Winston Churchill had nothing to do with this movement and it wanted nothing to do with him. The Peace Pledge enthusiasts were scared by his demands for major rearmament programmes. He was seen as a warmonger. Yet his reading of Hitler's intentions was not always inspired. He too could be wrong. As late as 1937, less than twelve months before Munich, he wrote: 'I declare my belief that a major war is not imminent, and I still believe there is a good chance of no major war taking place in our time.' At the time it did not strike me as all that different from Chamberlain's own optimism that he might somehow persuade Hitler to preserve peace.

DOMINATING BUT IMPOTENT

Notwithstanding the events described above, both Lloyd George and Winston Churchill dominated Parliament throughout the thirties. But they were powerless; almost totally impotent in influencing events. They delivered the most wonderful speeches, and were brilliant men of enormous world stature. But they never acted together, they never took joint action on any major issue; the brutal truth was that nobody would follow either. They never had a common front. Lloyd George had only his family group of daughter Megan and son Gwilym, with very few operational links with the Liberals. Winston Churchill had only his minute personal following. Yet here is the paradox of Churchill's powerlessness. L. G. had far more close, intimate, and regular contacts with the liberal-minded Tories of the rising generation like Macmillan and his friends than Churchill ever had. The 'New Deal' types of progressive Conservatives were attracted to Lloyd George by the dynamic appeal of his economic, financial, and public works programme to relieve the depression. But Churchill was not interested in economic and social problems, which he saw was an encroachment on politics. In consequence, his was a lone voice to campaign on defence. Lloyd George also had his own version of the Popular Front through his Council of Action groups, which embraced all parties and notably the Free Churches. Harold Macmillan appeared on Lloyd George's campaign platforms after resigning the Tory Whip in protest against his Government's treatment of the unemployed. His inclinations lay with Lloyd George not Winston.

THE FOCUS GROUP

About this time Churchill did have the makings of a wider-based grouping. It was entitled FOCUS; launched in 1935 on the theme of Freedom and Peace, linked with the Arms and the Covenant programme he had written. But this was a tiny little band. His main colleagues were his old friend Lady Violet Bonham Carter and Sir Archibald Sinclair (later Lord Thurso) of the Liberals. They lunched and dined as a select group in the Pinafore Room at the Savoy, not the natural setting for a movement to stir the masses. In the end the group simply melted away. Winston was too authoritarian. The crunch came at a rally organised for the Albert Hall to alert the Press and warn the country about the menace of Hitler. When Churchill arrived he announced he wanted to speak on the Abdication crisis then reaching its peak. Sir Walter Citrine (later Lord Citrine), general secretary of the TUC, had agreed to take the chair in order to focus attention on the plight of the trade union leaders under Hitler. He told Churchill that he would not preside if he insisted on bringing in the King, the Monarchy and Mrs Simpson. Churchill accepted Citrine's condition with bad grace. But FOCUS went into eclipse as a movement, while continuing with its principal adherents. As Churchill said: 'I've got no party base or backing, no platform, no Press, and, worst of all, I am without a following.'

He received scant support or sympathy from the various Left-of-Centre groupings and movements—the 'intelligentsia' of the period—which flourished in profusion in the thirties. After the bitter disillusionments of the Spanish civil war they complained that they could have done then with some support from Churchill warning the people about the menace of Hitler and Mussolini using Spain as operational training for their bombers, tanks and supply organisations.

Spain did not move Churchill deeply. His attitude on Mussolini and the Italian invasions of Abyssinia and Albania was criticised as equivocal. He was not allowed to forget that in the early days of Fascism he said in the Italian papers that he was impressed and charmed by Mussolini's 'gentle and simple bearing and by his calm detached poise', and complimented the Fascist leader on 'producing order, stability and patriotism' and providing the 'antidote to the Communist poison'.

Communism preoccupied his mind obsessively in the early years. 'Kill the Bolshie and kill the Hun' was his line according to Lady Violet Bonham Carter; he had wanted to treat Germany generously in order to get rid of the menace of militant Communism and avoid the resurgence of Germany's Prussian militarism. When Hitler became Chancellor in January 1933, and the Reichstag went up in flames, he wasted no time in identifying the danger to mankind and human freedom everywhere. Earlier he was convinced that the greatest danger to mankind lay in 'The Red Peril'. Hitler changed all that. But even after Munich many of the most powerful forces supporting Chamberlain, notably the City, big business and the upper social world, remained convinced that Russian Communism and not German Nazism represented the biggest menace to Britain and the Empire.

The true measure of Churchill's isolation, and the extent to which even powerful forces hostile to Chamberlain's appeasement deliberately kept him at arm's length, was exposed when Anthony Eden resigned as Foreign Secretary from the Chamberlain Government in February 1938. As described in Chapter 1 the glow of hindsight reflects Eden's action as inspired by a defiant anti-appeasement challenge, the final break with a policy he could no longer tolerate. Not quite so. The immediate reasons were more complex: concern for pride and status predominating. Eden resented Chamberlain going behind his back to contact Mussolini and snubbing a peace initiative by President Roosevelt without consulting him at the Foreign Office. He had complained that Baldwin took no interest in foreign affairs, then he complained that Chamberlain interfered too much, in short that the latter wanted to be his own Foreign Secretary and to treat the incumbent as an executant of the PM's decisions. (In his resignation speech Eden was very low key and passive, almost apologetic, in sharp contrast to the 'surrender to blackmail' vehemence of Lord Cranborne, later the Marquis of Salisbury, Eden's No. 2.)

Anthony Eden was enormously popular in the Conservative Party and throughout the country, with a strong following among the then numerous Liberal Party and Labour's nonconformist element, then very strong in the constituencies. On the division which took place on his resignation twenty five Tory MPs refused to vote for their Prime Minister. This was the first real revolt against appeasement. In power terms this should have been the beginning of a major re-grouping. Like most of the other political correspondents at the time, I was writing that the next likely development was the emergence of a new Right-of-Centre Popular Front, with Eden and Churchill at its head—in that order. Such a realignment in British politics in the months preceding Munich would have had a profound impact on the sequence of events which led to the outbreak of war. But Anthony Eden made no attempt to link arms with Winston Churchill. He kept his distance. There was no unity, no common front, no agreement on joint action between them.

NO SUPPORT FROM EDEN

Even after Hitler annexed Austria in March 1938, only a month after Eden's resignation, and six months before the Czech crisis and Munich, they shared broadly identical views but did not share or seek unity. The explanation for this lies in the history of Churchill's isolation. Eden was the creature, the creation, of the Conservative Party. Ever since the early twenties he had been worshipped in the party as the Prince Charming, like a matinée idol of the inter-war years, its *beau ideal* of what every Young Conservative should be and look like. So when he split with Chamberlain his first priority was to preserve party unity. Many times he left the impression that his second priority was to get back into the bosom of Tory power as soon as ever he could find a suitable formula for reconciliation. Churchill, on the other hand, was regarded as a renegade, the big menace to Conservative unity and its leadership. Eden was old enough to remember Baldwin's description of Lloyd George in 1921 at the famous Carlton Club meeting: 'It is owing to that dynamic force and that personality that the Liberal Party has been smashed to pieces . . .

and it is my firm conviction that the same thing will happen to our Party
... until it is smashed to atoms and lost in ruins.' The overwhelming
mass of Tories were terrified that Churchill would bring the same catastrophe to their party as Lloyd George had brought to the once great
Liberal Party.

As late in the day as 1939 the completeness of Churchill's isolation and
loneliness was demonstrated by some startling comparisons in a public
opinion poll on leadership rivalries conducted by the British Institute of
Public Opinion published in the *News-Chronicle* eight months *after*
Munich and only four months *before* the outbreak of war. The poll asking
people about Tory leadership was confined to Government supporters
only, in order to exclude any artificial weighting factor by Labour opinion. The figures confirmed that thirty-eight per cent of Tory voters said
they wanted Eden as party leader and Prime Minister if Chamberlain
retired or resigned. Only seven per cent mentioned Churchill as their
choice. Given the thirty-eight per cent support for Eden and the thirty-six
per cent who could not contemplate Chamberlain going in any case,
Churchill's standing was derisory. No wonder he wrote at the time: 'I feel
alone.'

This explains why Churchill was never admitted to the Eden group,
comprising some thirty to forty MP critics of Chamberlain, which had
formed around their idol. They met regularly every week at the London
home of Ronald Tree, a rich young Conservative member who had mar-
ried an American heiress, so he was well able to provide the setting, hospi-
tality, and the security from Tory Whips' spies. But Winston was never
associated with Anthony's disciples. Harold Macmillan was a founder
member of the Eden group along with all the other liberal-minded progressive young Conservatives (derided by the Conservative Whips as 'the
glamour boys'). They identified with Eden, just as they had identified
with Lloyd George. But while full of ardour for much that Churchill was
saying, they never identified with him. Even Duff Cooper, when he cour-
ageously resigned from the Cabinet within hours of Chamberlain's
Munich deal with Hitler, joined the Eden group. Neither was Churchill a
member of the equally active group led by Leo Amery. He was thus exposed as the dangerous fellow nobody wanted to know.

MUNICH AND AFTER

In this study of Winston Churchill in the inter-war years, portrayed as far
from the folk hero promoted by legend, the night of Munich must be seen
as the climacteric. It not only made the Second World War inevitable, it
exposed the final tearful humiliation for Winston Churchill. For it revealed in the cruellest fashion that even his closest friends and supporters

no longer trusted his judgment and were not prepared to be identified with him in his final warning to Chamberlain. As the Prime Minister flew off to Munich to sign the final surrender terms, Churchill met with his little personal following, again in the Pinafore Room at the Savoy, for their regular luncheon party. Winston insisted on drafting a telegram to be sent to Chamberlain warning him against making any further concessions to Hitler and adding the ultimatum that if he did so he would face a hostile and angry House of Commons on his return. The intention was to make the message all-party by getting Clem Attlee, Labour Party leader, Anthony Eden, Sir Archibald Sinclair, the Liberal leader, Lord Hugh Cecil, representing the nation's conscience through the League of Nations Union, and Sir Walter Citrine to sign in support of the final protest and warning. Winston and his group dispersed for the afternoon, confident that they would have this influential roll-call to add to the message by the time they met again for dinner. Their confidence was that such a widely-supported demonstration covering every sector of British opinion would restrain Chamberlain from making any more concessions and prevent him from sacrificing Czechoslovakia as a peace-offering.

When the tiny group met at the Savoy in the evening Churchill discovered that nobody wanted to be associated with his message. The last great initiative in an effort to save Europe and the world from war collapsed before it started. Eden refused to have his name added to the telegram because, he said, it would be seen as an act of hostility to Chamberlain—an extraordinary excuse by one who had resigned from the Chamberlain Cabinet only months previously. The lack of courage and support from Eden should not have been all that surprising; Winston once described 'dear Anthony' as a 'lightweight'. One of the oddest features of all during the sordid appeasement period, to my mind, was that Eden never once identified himself with any attacks on Chamberlain's policies in the country. On the night of Munich itself the commitment to party unity prevailed in his mind. Attlee brushed Churchill's overtures aside because, he said, the Labour conference was due in a fortnight's time and he would prefer not to commit the party to any such telegram in advance. The TUC leadership declined to sign because it might pre-empt a Labour Party decision. Thus they all peeled off; nobody was prepared to sign the Churchill draft. So the threat about the all-party fury awaiting the Prime Minister in Parliament had to be blue-pencilled out from the proposed message to Munich, leaving only the sentence appealing to the Premier not to make any sacrifices affecting another nation's independence to the German Führer. In the end the telegram was never sent.

Lady Violet Bonham Carter later gave this heart-rending picture of the humiliated and abandoned Churchill when he realised the full agony of his loneliness and the magnitude of the desertions: 'Winston remained seated in his chair, frozen, like a man of stone. I saw the tears in his eyes. I could feel the iron entering his soul. His last attempt to salvage what was left of honour and good faith had failed.'* The day after, on Chamberlain's return, he made himself the most detested man in the Conservative Party when he ridiculed the mass euphoria by stating in his Commons speech: 'We have sustained a total and unmitigated defeat . . . This is only the first sip of a bitter cup which will be proffered us year by year.' If the telegram had been sent as drafted by Churchill and supported by Attlee, Eden, Citrine and the others, would General Halder have been prepared to carry out his long-prepared coup against Hitler? This is the greatest imponderable of all.

After Munich Chamberlain came under enormous pressure from the party organisation to submit his policies to the country in an election, seeking the people's endorsement. He would almost certainly have been returned by a landslide, with a mandate to carry on with his programme of appeasing the dictators and avoiding war; too many families retained acute memories of the First World War and had no wish to see the new generation decimated as well. There was widespread relief in the Labour Party at the political deliverance when the Prime Minister let it be known through a few of us in the Lobby that he had no desire to capitalise on his obvious popularity. An election would have posed great problems for Churchill. He could not with credibility stand as a Conservative candidate pledged to support a Prime Minister and a Government's policies which he despised. And to stand as an independent Conservative would have invited annihilation.

He did not know it but plans were being discussed at the highest levels in the party to relieve him of such a dilemma of conscience and loyalty. The intention was to disown him at constituency level, by seeking a new candidate pledged to support the Prime Minister and his Government. This would have compelled Winston to fight as an Independent Tory or more probably as a Constitutionalist, the identity he preferred when previously in the wilderness in the early twenties, when he was between turning his back on the Liberals and seeking sanctuary with the Conservatives. Just how close he came to excommunication he never knew. Had Hitler not invaded Poland when he did, by the spring of 1940 Churchill might have found himself opposed by an official pro-Chamberlain Conservative candidate. And that would have meant the loss of his seat at Epping and the end of Churchill in Parliament.

* *Winston Churchill as I Knew Him*, Violet Bonham Carter (Collins).

First moves in the campaign to isolate him officially came on 5 February, 1939. In his Epping constituency Colonel Sir Colin Thornton-Kemsley, chairman of the Chigwell Conservative Association, fired the first shot. He said: 'Many of the Branch associations in the division are in practically open revolt against the member. They demand a candidate who will support the Prime Minister and the National Government in place of a member who, while he does not hesitate to shelter under the goodwill attaching to the name of a great party, constantly, and almost it seems inevitably, criticises the policy and actions of the party's leader.'

Just to prove that this was not an accidental off-the-cuff or impetuous warning to Churchill, delivered without consultation in high places, Colonel Thornton-Kemsley—the knighthood came after—returned to the theme a month later at another constituency party meeting, spelling out a warning in even greater detail and with even greater authority. For these are his words verbatim, carefully prepared:

> Mr Churchill's post-Munich insurrection was shocking. His deplorable broadcast to the USA was about as helpful to this country as Mr Loyd George's writing to the Hearst Press at the time of the general strike.
>
> His castigation of the National Government which we returned him to support was a mockery and a sham which in any other party but the Conservative Party would have earned his immediate expulsion.
>
> Loyal Conservatives in Epping have been placed in an intolerable position.
>
> Unless Mr Churchill is prepared to work for the National Government and the Prime Minister, he ought no longer to shelter under the will and name of such a great party. Most of us in Epping Division agree that Mr Churchill has overstepped the line.*

There is not the slightest doubt that when Thornton-Kemsley served notice on Churchill that he was in imminent danger of being kicked out of the Conservative Party he was specially chosen by the Tory Establishment determined to be rid of Winston. His role was not confined to Churchill in Epping. In a book of memoirs he wrote thirty-six years later he* made an astonishing confession. It appears that in the summer of 1938 'James Stuart (Deputy Chief Whip and Scottish Whip) asked me to meet him at the House. Over drinks on the terrace he told me that the Unionists in Kinross and West Perthshire were exasperated by the constant criticisms of the Government she was elected to support by their member, Katherine Duchess of Atholl ... The executive committee wished, under conditions of the strictest secrecy, to select a more acceptable candidate to represent the constituency at the next election. Would I meet the members of a small selection committee to discuss the position

* *Through Winds & Tides*, C. Thornton-Kemsley (Standard Press, Montrose).

with them.' He did. He was found most acceptable, and was in process of being lined up for the seat. But the Duchess discovered the secret ploy to disown her. She pre-empted the situation by immediately applying for the Chiltern Hundreds, determined to force a by-election. In these circumstances an unknown outsider like Thornton-Kemsley would have stood no chance and the Tories rushed in a local farmer, McNair Snadden, and local loyalties defeated the Duchess narrowly a few days before Christmas 1938.

The Duchess of Atholl is brought into my story as highly relevant to what was being plotted for Churchill in Epping. During the Spanish civil war she proved such a vehement critic of the Government's non-interventionist line that we all started referring to her as the 'Red Duchess'.

Her defeat in Perthshire provided a perfect precedent to reinforce the assault against Winston Churchill in Epping. She was the test case. If she could be liquidated so easily, then Churchill could be toppled by similar tactics. By then he was in a desperate, even indefensible situation. He sent the Duchess an enthusiastic message, extolling her courage and appealing for voters to back her. James Stuart was a central character. He had a double remit: as Scottish Whip he was responsible for disposing of the 'Red Duchess'; as Deputy Chief Whip he shared the official desire to dump Churchill in Epping. In his own book of memoirs* Stuart told many years afterwards of the sensitive tensions felt on both sides when Churchill (by then Prime Minister) asked him, with no great enthusiasm, to become his Chief Government Whip. Churchill and he had what Winston in his own phrasing would have described as 'a little bother'—'I would prefer to call it a head-on collision clash, with strong words on both sides,' wrote Stuart. Beyond that not a clue to what he had really said to Churchill. Or what the great man said in reply. The curtain of discretion and secrecy came down. But fortunately Churchill, in his zeal as a correspondent, kept the record straight. Thanks to the research by the historian and biographer Martin Gilbert, what Stuart really said to Churchill is no longer a mystery and proves that, after the defeat of the Duchess, the Government and party leaders became more aggressive and self-confident in their Churchill hunt. Here it should be stressed by one who knew him well for forty years that Stuart was not the type of politician ever to go out on a political limb without first being certain that he was solidly supported by the party's hierarchy. Martin Gilbert records in his book that Churchill wrote to a family friend of long standing: 'James Stuart had the cheek to tell me in his exultation about the Duchess's defeat that I ought not to accept the Whip any longer. I naturally told him

* *Within the Fringe*, Viscount Stuart of Findhorn (Bodley).

to go to hell, or Epping.'*

Three aspects of this belligerent request by Stuart require emphasis. First, to ask a member to give up the Whip is to ask him, in Winston's language, to get to hell out of the party. Second, Stuart had little status in the party hierarchy and it is inconceivable that he would have been so challenging to Churchill unless he knew for certain he had the backing of the Prime Minister and his Chief Whip, Captain Margesson. Third, Perthshire was obviously regarded as a warming-up exercise for Epping.

Back at Epping events were moving forward inexorably to dispose of Churchill by similar methods of secrecy and orchestrated revolt as had effectively disposed of the 'Red Duchess'. After the initial ranging shots by Thornton-Kemsley mentioned above, the moves to isolate Winston were intensified. He was alive to the dangers. Indeed, he forecast that Hitler might try to force Chamberlain into an election, pledged 'to deliver the goods' and to get rid of troublesome Churchill about whom Hitler was frequently protesting in his major speeches. So Churchill moved in and demanded a meeting of the council of the constituency association, when he got a big majority. Three decades later Thornton-Kemsley recalled in his book that the anti-Churchillites became incensed and proposed an ultimatum to their MP: 'Either moderate your criticisms of the Government you were elected to support, or stand, when the time comes, as an Independent Conservative.' A clear invitation to commit political suicide. They even invited Sir Thomas Fowell Buxton, Baronet, local landowner and Establishment bigwig, to accept nomination as the official Conservative candidate. He declined. The fear was that a split vote, while certain to cost Churchill the seat, would present it to the Liberals.

Another meeting of the constituency party was held in the spring of 1939 and this time Churchill survived by a touch-and-go majority. The critics then set out to capture control of the key constituency branches like Waltham Abbey, Nazeing, Theydon Bois, Chigwell, and Epping. So after Churchill's narrow squeak in the spring the next full meeting of the constituency council in the early winter would have seen him disowned and discredited, or forced to surrender on terms which he of all people could never accept. And the mandate would have been given to the selection committee to find an acceptable loyalist candidate for the general election, then provisionally set for the spring of 1940.

This danger of being repudiated by his own constituency was never far from his mind when he discovered the scale of the operation being mounted against him. To historian Ramsay Muir he wrote at the time stating that if his own constituency were to turn against him—by that he meant the Conservative Party organisation—he would fight back in a by-

* *Winston Churchill*, Vol V, Martin Gilbert (Heinemann).

election. By mentioning a by-election and not the general election he indicated clearly that if the party machine decided not to adopt him again and to seek an official pro-Chamberlain Tory instead he was ready to repeat the defiance of the Duchess of Atholl, by resigning his seat and fighting the resultant by-election. In another letter (29 October 1938), traced by biographer Martin Gilbert's volume quoted earlier, he posed the question whether 'it is all to go down the drain as it did in the India business through the influence of the Central Office and Government Whips? If so, I know my duty.' The pro-appeasement anti-Churchill coup, he apprehended, was as close as that. Churchill escaped from this repudiation thanks to Hitler's attack on Poland in September 1939. In those crucial pre-war months Churchill was only too well aware of the strenuous plans in hand to unseat him.

It was at around this time that I was overtaken by the saga. During the period that Thornton-Kemsley was leading the campaign to dump Churchill, and about the same time as the Duchess of Atholl purge, a by-election was created in Kincardine and West Aberdeenshire by the appointment of the sitting member, Sir Malcolm Barclay-Harvey, to be Governor of South Australia. As my old daily paper, the *Aberdeen Press and Journal*, was within my journalistic bailiwick in those days as part of the Kemsley (later Thomson) empire, I was anxious to discover who the new Tory candidate was likely to be. Late one night, after the House of Commons rose, I met Chief Whip Captain Margesson and his second-in-command James Stuart in the Lobby, walking towards their Whips' suite of offices.

I asked them if they could tell me the likely identity of the new candidate falling heir to the traditionally safe party seat. Or, if not, could they give me the names of the three most likely for the short list.

'There's only to be one,' replied Margesson. 'He's Colin Thornton-Kemsley. He's our chairman out in Epping.'

At the moment I wondered whether I was to have in my territorial flock a relative of my proprietor, the first Viscount Kemsley. So I asked Margesson and Stuart if there were family ties and why someone totally unknown in the North and in public life there was being presented with such a political plum.

Margesson replied that Thornton-Kemsley was no relative of the Kemsley newspaper family, and added that he was to get the seat because he was doing splendid work in Epping for the party and in particular helping 'to fix Churchill' as an enemy of the Prime Minister.

I duly phoned my report to Aberdeen, giving the name of the candidate certain to be the next MP for the constituency, and proceeded on my journey homewards. But at Westminster underground station, waiting to catch the tube to Victoria, I was overtaken by two breathless Whips' messengers. 'Thank God we've caught you,' they exclaimed. 'Come back at once. Margesson and Stuart are throwing fits about you.'

By then the Houses of Parliament were in darkness, except for the lights in the Whips' corridor, where I found Margesson and Stuart pacing up and down.

'Can you kill that story about Thornton-Kemsley before it appears?' demanded Margesson.

'I can still just stop it,' I replied. 'But why the sudden change? Has he turned the seat down?'

'Nothing like that. But we've forgotten to tell the local Chairman of the Unionist Association in the constituency that it's got to be Thornton-Kemsley. Hold the report for twenty-four hours for God's sake. James (Stuart) will phone in the morning. Then you run the story for all it's worth as official.'

I recall the incident in some detail not only because it confirms how very close Churchill's leading critic in the constituency was to the party's leadership but also to indicate the autocratic management of the party's affairs which decided the selection of party candidates without any of the latter-day procedures about local democracy and constituency independence. At the time it was widely understood that Thornton-Kemsley was egged on by Margesson and several of Chamberlain's Ministers to mount a campaign to overthrow Churchill—he resided in the Epping constituency and owned a major surveying business—and had also been their first choice to overwhelm the unwelcome Duchess.

Thornton-Kemsley won the by-election in Kincardine and West Aberdeenshire comfortably in March 1939, but the general election in 1945 was a different story, and is recalled here because of the fresh light it shed on the attempted *putsch* against Churchill six and seven years previously. John Junor, the Liberal candidate, taunted Thornton-Kemsley with double standards in political loyalties, winning the by-election in 1939 on an anti-Churchill pro-appeasement coupon and then trying to win at the general election in 1945 by cashing in on Winston's popularity. Junor revealed for the first time some of the Epping secrets and how his opponent had organised the strenuous efforts to unseat Churchill before the war. Thornton-Kemsley, needled by this flash-back into his past, protested against his opponent's tactics and claimed that except for differences over Munich he had been a foremost supporter of the great man all his life. Junor's disclosures made an instant impact, and he just failed to bring off one of the sensations of the election: he lost by a slender 642 votes in a poll of over 21,000.

Junor's exposé rankled for a long time, and even in 1974 Thornton-

Kemsley reopened the old sores by trying, in his book mentioned above, to score off his old critic. 'I had a straight fight with Lieutenant John Junor of the Fleet Air Arm, a former President of Glasgow University Liberal Club, who was later to become a director of the Beaverbrook Press*—an unhappy fate for a promising young Liberal . . . In the last three days of an otherwise genteel and uneventful contest my opponent thought fit to raise the matter of my pre-war disagreement with Mr Churchill and by inference to cast doubt upon my loyalty to him. I explained the circumstances. . . . I described our reconciliation on the outbreak of war.'

Thornton-Kemsley claimed that the letter of 'reconciliation' from Churchill was among his most treasured possessions, but for the full flavour of Winston's reactions to the letter of apology for ever trying to unseat him we had to wait for Martin Gilbert's passing reference in his official biography of the great man. Most of the thousands of letters sent to Winston Churchill when he became Prime Minister in 1940 were never put before him. 'But Mrs Hill [his personal secretary] put this one on his desk with the message "*Please* read this" and he did so. He also showed it to his wife and read it over the telephone to Sir James Hawkey.† Then, on September 13, he replied, accepting Thornton-Kemsley's apology, and adding: "I certainly think that Englishmen ought to start fair with one another from the outset in so grievous a struggle and so far as I am concerned the past is dead."'

As ever, Churchill displayed magnanimity. But he was never in any doubt about the gravity of the attempts made to overthrow him in Epping. He discussed with friends what his attitude might have to be if Chamberlain had rushed an election in order to prove to Hitler that he 'could deliver the goods'. The danger to Churchill was miraculously and mercifully avoided by Hitler's attack on Poland. But for that, Winston Churchill may never have been available in Parliament to assume the highest office in the darkest hour. It was a close-run destiny.

The general election due in the spring of 1940 was avoided by statutory enactment (postponing the election until the end of the war), by which time Churchill had become Prime Minister. And Britain stood alone.

* John Junor went on to become the doyen of Fleet Street editors, with his record-breaking run as editor of the *Sunday Express*.

† He was Churchill's most loyal supporter in the constituency even when the tide of anti-Churchill bitterness seemed on the point of sweeping away the member's meagre defences.

9

THE LOBBY

In 1884 the House of Commons passed a resolution establishing the right of 'a gentleman of the Press' to enter the Members' Lobby to talk to Ministers and MPs. (The House of Lords caught up eighty years later!) The Lobby List, the sacred scrolls kept by the Serjeant-at-Arms, Parliament's chief executive and ceremonial officer, on which are recorded the names of journalists nominated by editors to be their political reporters, started up in 1885. Thus the mystique of the Lobby was born. The show has been running ever since, with scarcely a word changed in the script. The Lobby still operates from the rectangular lobby immediately outside the Commons chamber, whence it derived its name. Not that the 1884 initiative was inspired by any ideals for more open Government. Its purpose was to create a new group of insiders and exclude the public and the mass of writers for the countless newsletters, pamphlet-sheets and weeklies who had overcrowded the Members' Lobby.

There is a finely drawn distinction here between *de jure* and *de facto* recognition of the Lobby. Though the official Parliamentary records mention 1884 and 1885, all the available Press evidence really pinpoints the date of birth as 1881. Confirmation of this rests within the author's own knowledge. In 1931 two of the founding fathers, R. G. Emery, of the *Morning Post*, and Alexander Mackintosh, of the *Aberdeen Free Press* and later of the *Liverpool Post*, were entertained in style at Westminster on completing fifty years *in* the Lobby as accredited Lobby correspondents.

OUTSIDERS ON THE INSIDE

For close on a century the mysteries of 'Lobby terms', which critics deride as the mumbo-jumbo of a secret society, have prevailed unimpaired and virtually unamended. Lobby terms, the despair of all the Lobby's enemies but now widely adopted as their very own by countless

groups of specialist journalists everywhere, enable Lobby men and women to report as their own views and discoveries the opinions and possible policies of Prime Ministers and others confided to them—not at some metaphysical level but physically at meetings in a Commons committee room, never to be acknowledged by the Minister concerned. They know better than anybody they are playing a game of compulsory kite flying by reporting the views of high authorities anonymously and unattributably after communion with the political saints. The Lobby correspondents are the most important and influential corps in the whole of the modern media as a source of important news, political investigation and comment. Their constant challenge is to assert their independence and not to appear the allies and part of the established Executive on whom they depend for their daily sustenance.

Here an important distinction must be established. Lobby correspondents must not be confused with lobbyists, who are of a totally different kidney. Lobbyists belong to the vast new army of public relations consultants, advisers and contact men—the hidden persuaders—who influence and sometimes pressurise politicians to support, amend or oppose Government policies of major or minor importance on behalf of powerful and well-britched outside organisations. Though eyebrows may legitimately be raised about the expense-account liberality involved in promotion, such measures should be regarded as inevitable in an era when Whitehall policies and Departmental administrative decisions affect public life and private interests at all levels. Washington remains the pre-eminent example of how the gravy train and the pork barrel prevail in a political world dominated by the PR expertise. At Westminster I have seen some examples of such campaigns, but in my experience the most notable example of high-pressure commercial lobbying in this country was the campaign which captured Parliament and public opinion for commercial television. In my judgment this remains the classic illustration of how in modern power politics a well-oiled campaign can overcome all obstacles.

Such lobbying is entirely alien to the Lobby correspondent's primary mission in life, which is to discover the mass of information which Governments want to suppress, manage, control or delay. It is impossible to understand how the Lobby system works without first recognising the magnitude of the official Information Service which has been created in Whitehall. For the first loyalty of the Service is to its masters not to Fleet Street and the media, while the first loyalty of Fleet Street and the Lobby is to discover and disclose the other side's most strongly defended secrets. This is at the heart of the secrecy of power and the politics of secrecy.

There was only one Press Officer in the whole of Whitehall when I first arrived at Westminster in the early nineteen-thirties. He was George Steward, who had been appointed by Ramsay MacDonald, then Prime Minister, to the staff of No 10 Downing Street as an additional 'Private Secretary (Intelligence)'. His official remit was to provide liaison between the Lobby/Political correspondents and the Government, but his personal role was to plug the numerous leaks taking place from MacDonald's National Government (then formed from three parties, the ideal political mix for malicious and inspired leaking). That was how the incestuous relationships between Government and Lobby on an organised and corporate basis started. From this initial move to centralise and institutionalise outside contacts has grown today's mammoth apparatus of power, information and news-management now at the disposal of all Governments as they come and go and as the Executive in Whitehall goes on forever. At the latest count there were close on 1,500 Press and Information Officers on the State's payroll. Even they formed but part of the vast State apparatus. For communications and information services have become very big business in modern Government, by far the most powerful weapon at the disposal of the State not merely to inform but to *influence* people's minds, as we shall see. The Information budget totals £50 million; its advertising programmes to keep people informed of official policies come to £15 million.

A massive increase in information officers does not of course guarantee an increased flow of information. Having played a minor role in the early midwifery strains which gave birth to today's giant, one can only marvel at the manner in which communications have become such an enormous and complex arm of Government and that the Lobby has preserved its integrity and professional independence despite the occupational hazards in a world where, it has been said, 'honest men lie and decent men cheat for power' in order to manipulate and exploit the media.

Once the power potential of the George Steward experiment at No. 10 was recognised by Government and Executive no time was lost in exploiting the breakthrough. Throughout the thirties, forties and fifties the first generation of Whitehall's Press and information officers were progressively appointed to all the Ministries. Then they shared one primary purpose. This was to provide a new direct contact between Government and the Lobby. This development has had many consequences over the years. First, it established Information as an arm of Government. Secondly, it revolutionised the Lobby system for political journalists at Westminster from its former individualistic independence to the formalised, centralised group basis of today. In the process, largely because of its specialised and confidential contacts behind the scenes, it has acquired a mystique all its own, even seen as an underground Mafia. Its numerous critics see it as a sinister secret society. In particular, Lobby correspondents are derided as the lackeys of the Government of the day, co-operating eagerly with the politicians in the new sophisticated techniques of news-management and thus partners with the Government in the manipulation of public opinion. In short, that they possess a vested interest in a system which guarantees them a privileged role within the Establishment. The charge was summed up in a single sentence by Tony Wedgwood Benn when he described the Government and Lobby as a 'partnership in suppression which really damages the public interest'. This was Benn 'on the record', of course. The author and some colleagues on the beat never found him wanting when it came to 'off the record' contacts in commenting with barbed sincerity on the welfare of some comrades in the same Cabinet or National Executive. As for the 'lackeys' sneer, I should be surprised if former Premiers like Harold Macmillan, Harold Wilson, Edward Heath and Alex Douglas-Home found the Lobby journalists at all complaisant and understanding in their news-reporting when the great men were in travail and eclipse, facing final overthrow.

THE MYSTIQUE

The Lobby's mysterious ways and influences, always off-stage in the grand theatre of politics, have an irresistible fascination for politico-academics and college lecturers on current affairs who have often tried to describe the system from the *outside*. The irony is that the most persistent critics of the Lobby are those elsewhere in the media, as well as academics in political science who depend on the initiative and daily writings by Westminster's political correspondents for their knowledge of contemporary political history. They rely on the Westminster Corps for their living. It is time that the distortions were disposed of and the history and role of the Lobby within the complex Government-Whitehall-Parliament system was put on the record *from the inside*. When I first entered the scene in the early thirties my predecessor on the Aberdeen papers, Sir Alexander Mackintosh, was still around regularly to give advice and guidance to the youngster newly arrived from the far north. He joined the Press Gallery and Lobby when the precincts were first opened to the provincial Press in 1881. So between us our shared experience covers the Lobby's first century.

Perhaps Macaulay is indirectly responsible for the most persistent myth which has dogged the Lobby over the years. When in 1828 he described the Parliamentary reporters then officially admitted to the Press Gallery for the first time as the new 'Fourth Estate' of the realm he was referring to the new dimension Parliament then acquired by the presence of the newsmen in an historical concept, by guaranteeing 'Open Parliament'. This identity has proved a handicap for the political correspondents. The most constant indictment by the critics is that Lobbymen identify themselves as part of the Establishment, partners sharing power, authority and special knowledge with the three hallowed 'Estates of the Realm' like the Lords Spiritual, Lords Temporal, and Commons. Here lies the greatest danger, when newsmen regard themselves as honorary members of the power Establishment and *ex officio* members of the political system and forget their primary adversary relationship with Premiers, Cabinets and Executive—and never as allies, legmen and buddies.

It is a small move from a flattering status of being 'accepted' to being viewed and used—and indeed all too often *exploited*—as the Fourth Arm of the Government, sharing the honours and burdens of power. This relationship is dangerous and misleading, for it ignores the basic purposes of the Press and the media: to discover, investigate and reveal those policies, splits and decisions which all Governments of all parties want to conceal. For secrecy is essential to Governments and especially to Whitehall's bureaucracy, as the key to the mystery of power. The interests of Government and Press are irreconcilable and the healthiest relationship must be one of tension, mutual suspicion, and constant hostility. For to do their jobs successfully, each depends and feeds upon the other, bound up in the bundle of life together in a delicate and tricky relationship of checks and balances on which a free and open society must rest.

But where precisely to balance this elusive relationship? Iain Macleod, who was not backward in organising his own 'Lobby within the Lobby' with four trusted friends to receive weekly his private guidance on policies and colleagues, believed that relations are best kept 'abrasive'. For myself I prefer 'adversary', for in this relationship neither deceives the other about the conflict in their roles 'in the national interest'.

This relationship between Government and the media concentrated in the Lobby is unique in the Western world, circumscribed and made inevitable as it is by the Official Secrets Act, the Privy Councillor's Oath, and Parliamentary Privilege. Each needs and feeds upon the other, neither is over-scrupulous or mealy-mouthed in exploiting the other, one offers publicity and fame, the other the highly marketable commodity of news and power. Both Government and the media are compelled by the unlimited demands of modern communications to co-operate, yet by all basic tests they are opposing and rival forces. I am convinced that if both Government and Press-TV-Radio are to do their jobs properly at Westminster and in Whitehall the 'adversary' situation is absolutely necessary, each eyeing the other with relentless suspicion yet retaining a mutual

129

tolerance and understanding of the other's needs, priorities and motives. This conflict is necessary, desirable and inevitable, and provided there is mutual respect this is the only way to strike the delicate and elusive balance on which a modern free society can alone function.

The danger comes when relations are too cosy and comfortable. Harold Wilson started off his long Premiership in this style, sometimes even appearing himself to be a Lobbyman *ex officio*, 'one of us', so perceptively sharp were his news judgments. In this period of rapture he described the magic of 'on Lobby terms' as 'an essential thread of precious metal in our Parliamentary democracy'. The intimate love-hate affair broke down eventually and inevitably in mutual angry recriminations when the Lobby corps complained that he was manipulating them, albeit with flair and brilliance, as a weapon of Government: using them as allies. Ever afterwards he was obsessed with a Press phobia and persecution complex. Neville Chamberlain was precisely the same, even complaining about the Press's 'betrayal and disloyalty' after he had blatantly news-managed the Lobby for years on his appeasement politics. After being on the receiving end of Prime Ministers' flatteries and frowns for so many years, the author's judgment is emphatic: the nation's best interests in a free society can only be served in a love-hate temper relationship with its constant tension and clash of interest. Otherwise the vast communications apparatus of today becomes the apparatus of deception and cynical manipulation, not of basic news and impartial information.

This judgment is by no means a consequence of the massive size of today's communications. Lobbying played an active part behind the pioneer pamphleteering sheets of the seventeenth and eighteenth centuries and then in the endless variety of literary-political weeklies which blossomed in the nineteenth and early twentieth centuries. It was in the early eighteen-eighties that the Lobby correspondents as we know the breed today became officially respectable and acceptable. Before then writers for the countless newsletters and broadsheets used to crowd into the Westminster lobbies with the general public, and generous tippers were given special treatment and gossip by the doorkeepers. To bring order out of chaos Parliament introduced the mystique of the Lobby List, which ever since, for a hundred years, has governed the presence of the political correspondents at Westminster. In the earlier years entry to the Press Gallery (thence the Lobby) was restricted to the London morning and evening papers, ten times more numerous than today's tiny list of public prints. Then in 1881 selected English provincial papers, as well as Scottish, Irish and Welsh, were also admitted. In most cases papers had one reporter acting as Press Gallery as well as Lobby correspondent, and it was only after the First World War that they split into clearly identifiable species of the trade. The distinction is easily explained. The Parliamentary correspondents are concerned primarily with what happens on the floor of the House of Commons chamber (and the Lords, too) while the Lobby/Political correspondents are concerned with what goes on behind the scenes in Government, Whitehall, and political parties: the power battles, the web, woof and colour of politics.

FIRST LOBBY MAN

The first Lobby correspondent accepted as setting the modern style of reporting politics in close-up was Sir Henry Lucy (1843–1924). He started off at Westminster as chief of the Parliamentary staff of the *Daily News* in 1872 and wrote the daily news summary ('Sketch Writer' in modern jargon) to lighten the verbatim Gallery reports. He was, however, more interested in what was going on behind the scenes and not in the formal set-pieces on the floor of the House. So he branched out into regular newspaper lobbying in the style we have practised ever since. He pioneered the modern technique of making politics interesting for the general readers by personalising and interpreting great events as a columnist, writing about people and less about the boring drudgery of politics. He was the first newspaperman to establish social and intimate contacts with politicians. His success was due, it was said, 'to his sources and authority combined with lambent humour and probity'. He made politics fun and created a new journalism coinciding with the growth of a new mass readership created by compulsory state education. He was the first Westminster reporter to establish his own reputation in his own right. He wrote a weekly piece for *Punch* as 'Toby MP' from 1881 to 1916 and for *The Observer* for twenty-nine years. In my own time I overlapped with Herbert Sidebotham, the last brilliant exponent of such pseudonymous diversity. In the combined Press empire of the Berry brothers, the first Lords Camrose and Kemsley, he was 'Student of Politics' in the *Sunday Times*, 'Candidus' in the *Daily Sketch* and *Sunday Graphic*, and the Parliamentary feature writer and commentator every morning in the *Daily Telegraph*. For several years I fell heir to his 'Student of Politics' cover in the *Sunday Times* until signed names became the fashion.

For a long time the roles of politician and journalist were accepted as naturally complementary and interchangeable; in the days of tiny circulations—*The Times*, *Daily Telegraph*, *Morning Post* and others sold only a few thousand copies each—they were partners in a tight little world of their own, as inbred elitists. Most politicians got into the writing act, while leading political writers switched careers into politics. Disraeli, for instance, was the most polished and versatile of writers, using a series of pseudonyms to conceal his identity when writing polemical and scurrilous articles about his political enemies and party colleagues, even including anonymous editorials in *The Times*. Other famous national leaders practised the dual roles without embarrassment. I suppose Bonar Law was the last PM to exploit the poison pen technique. He wrote an angry article for *The Times*, attacking the settlement reached by his own Chancellor of the Exchequer, Stanley Baldwin, with the United States on war debts. He signed it: 'By a Colonial'. He lost, Baldwin won. Since then Premiers have not had to do the drudgery of writing themselves; there was no need, for instance, for Harold Wilson to write a *Times* editorial condemning his Chancellor, James Callaghan, or for Callaghan to draft a pseudonymous article criticising Denis Healey's shortcomings. Sophisticated leaking saves the hazards of syntax. And all PMs have their favourite pen pals in Fleet Street.

As the Lobby succeeded in creating its own identity and role many editors became in effect their own political correspondents. Earlier the most famous editor of *The Times*, Delane, was such a regular attender at Westminster that he was treated more or less as an honorary member of Parliament. Later, from the turn of the century until the First World War, the famous Liberal editors like J. A. Spender, A. G. Gardiner, W. T. Stead, H. W. Massingham, did much of their own lobbying and political writing at first-hand. What distinguished this stage in Lobby development was that notable editors, Prime Ministers and leading politicians of those days met as equals, members of the same community and class, with shared background of public schools, Oxbridge, and social grouping. Distinguished journalists exerted as much influence by their private advice and judgment as colleagues in the same party as they did by their written words. The last Prime Minister in this relationship was Lloyd George, whose closest political advisers were Sir William Robertson Nicoll, editor of the *British Weekly*, and the unique C. P. Scott of the *Manchester Guardian*. In personal power terms, it was the golden age of editors, who were treated as partners and confidants.

The last of the line was probably Geoffrey Dawson, editor of *The Times*, who was happy to be the mouthpiece of Neville Chamberlain's ill-starred appeasement policies, a dreadful reminder of what happens to Press integrity when an editor becomes a political activist. He was not above slipping in and subbing out news reports in order to please mein Führer.

SELECTIVE LEAKING

Selective leaking, then and now, was and is the most sophisticated art of politics. It is impossible today to discover a refinement that has not been successfully tried out before. Take this example of a letter from a Cabinet

Minister to his Prime Minister. 'I think I ought to know who it is among my colleagues who deems me capable of what is not merely a gross indiscretion but a downright and discreditable breach of trust.' Who wrote it—Tony Wedgwood Benn, Denis Healey, William Whitelaw, Margaret Thatcher (to Edward Heath)? It was Lloyd George, in 1908 as Chancellor, protesting overmuch to Prime Minister Asquith about highly accurate leaks which appeared in the *Daily Chronicle* about pending Cabinet changes. They were inspired by L.G. himself to his favourite journalist.

There is nothing new under the sun in this Lobby-leaking business, enthusiastically encouraged by the newsmen (for it is their job to get news from the inside) and practised by one who became the greatest of Premiers for a variety of motives: to float kites, to test reactions to pending policies, to kill off policies before they are born by provoking hostile reactions, by malice aforethought to embarrass Ministerial colleagues—and of course to contribute to human knowledge and instant history from that morning's Cabinet! The Lloyd George letter confirms that in the early years of this century the newly emerging Lobby, when seeking to find a workable and acceptable system, was setting a hot pace.

As the era of the great political editors passed before the pressures of mass circulations, as well as the demands of managers and accountants, the new breed of Lobby/Political correspondents came into their own, divorcing themselves from the Press Gallery and establishing a new Press community in the corridors of power. They created for themselves the new role as news-gatherers and political commentators and feature writers. In the twenties and for most of the thirties the Lobby consisted of competing groups of twos and threes working together as warring syndicates. Two instances illustrate the set-up which was still working when I started on the Westminster beat. The Right-wing Imperialist *Morning Post* teamed up with the *Irish Independent* and the radical *Daily Chronicle*. In turn, the high Tory *Daily Telegraph* man formed his rival syndicate with the Liberal *Daily News* and the *Belfast Telegraph*, then close to the Carson-Birkenhead 'Ulster Will Fight' defiance. Similar permutations were numerous and widespread. This was perhaps the golden era of Lobby independence—independent of any formal or organised ties with Government, and largely independent of Fleet Street control, enjoying a unique form of Dominion status within the new Press empires then growing fat and prosperous.

One of the most persistent inaccuracies pictures the interwar Lobby as a small tiny outfit of a couple of dozen or so living a sheltered existence. Actually the detailed comparisons, within my own knowledge, between the early thirties and the eve of the eighties, confirm that basically the number of political journalists doing their highly specialised jobs has

133

remained more or less constant. Admittedly the increase in the number of alternates, deputies, and assistants has doubled the overall total, but this is primarily due to the mammoth flow of documents, reports, and official papers which cascade from Whitehall in unending volume. It is, however, in the type and character of Lobbying, news-gathering and daily reporting that the greatest revolution has taken place. This is the consequence of the decline in Britain's greatness as a world power which made Westminster the most important centre of international news in the world. Now, having lost an Empire and still seeking a role, Westminster has become home-based and inward-looking, concerned almost wholly with domestic affairs, which seldom justify visits by world newsmen in the old style. This in turn has transformed the old global dimensions of the Lobby. The caravan has moved on. As I remember Aneurin Bevan saying: 'Why read the crystal-ball when you can read the record.' So this is the record from the inside. It has its special importance, I hope, as reflecting a sector of national power and the world of communications little known and less understood beyond the Westminster corridors. Having been an activist and partisan in the Lobby system for so long one can claim the privilege of standing back, remembering where we have been, and speculating where we should be going.

THE LOBBY LIST
In the early nineteen-thirties there were forty-five full-time British Lobby correspondents representing UK papers and agencies on the Lobby List maintained by the Serjeant-at-Arms, the Speaker's main functionary at the House of Commons. That was the total strength of British political newsmen of the day. But they represented slightly less than half of the *total strength* of newspapermen admitted daily to the then Lobby. Of the grand total of ninety-two, slightly over twenty represented the old Empire and White Commonwealth: the leading Canadian, Australian, New Zealand and South African papers and agencies. Their roll-call is reminiscent of Britain's Imperial glory and Westminster's importance as the centre of news and power: the Australian Press Association, Australian Press Union, Argus South African Newspapers, Canadian Press, Southam Newspapers of Canada (mainly agencies and joint representation), the big papers of Toronto, Winnipeg, Melbourne, Sydney, Cape Town were individually represented by their own specialist writers. India had a strong team in the days of the British Raj from papers of the calibre of the *Statesman of Calcutta* and the *Times of India*. All were fortified by the Empire Press Union.

In addition, the Lobby was daily reinforced in its global coverage by the unique world character of the newsmen from the toughly competitive

American news agencies of the period, as well as the star international reporters from the *New York Times, Washington Post, Chicago Tribune*, and many others. The presence of the men and women from the leading Paris, Berlin, Amsterdam, Moscow, Rome, Zurich and Brussels dailies reflected the European importance of Westminster as the news-centre of world magnitude. Their names were not on the Lobby List as a formality or courtesy; they were in the Lobby daily in pursuit of hard news and opinion, lobbying intensively by personal contact with Prime Ministers and Ministers, Opposition leaders, the giants like Lloyd George and Winston Churchill, reinforced later as back-benchers by figures like Anthony Eden and Duff Cooper. The only difference between the UK and the international Press on the Lobby List was that the latter were not allowed to attend the occasional Lobby meetings of the British journalists, with the exception of one Australian, Trevor Smith, who first arrived at Westminster in 1922. Lobby meetings were most infrequent in those days, there was no group or corporate lobbying as it developed in the forties and fifties, when the new style of Lobbying became stylised.

The world nature of the Lobby in those pre-war days in turn exerted a direct influence on the British correspondents in two important respects. Having re-read old files at the Newspaper Library at Colindale my impression is confirmed that about fifty per cent of our writings (measured in news column inches), London Letters and feature articles, were on international and Imperial affairs and the endless succession of crises provoked by Hitler, Mussolini, Franco, Stalin and the Japanese invasion of Manchuria. Secondly, the daily competitive presence of the world's leading journalists provided an excellent stimulus and inspiration for the younger generation of UK Lobby newsmen like myself. (I should confess that I was handsomely treated by my seniors as the 'baby' throughout the 1930s and a little beyond, as good a training as anything to become its 'father' forty years on!) It also had the effect of providing us with wider international horizons and problems, a salutary check on obsessive preoccupation with one's own backyard. One further point illustrates how the status of the UK Press has been affected by Britain's retreat from world power. The overseas newspapermen paid the greatest attention to the editorial comments and independent reactions being taken by the great papers outside Fleet Street like the *Yorkshire Post, Manchester Guardian, Scotsman, Glasgow Herald* and *Birmingham Post*. Nightly during crisis periods the world correspondents waited eagerly for the editorial extracts from these papers for cabling overseas. The unique point was that some of these papers, although having little standing at home, enjoyed international importance. Today no attention is paid to what Leeds, Edinburgh, Glasgow, Birmingham and Manchester may say or think, because with the eclipse of Empire has come the eclipse of world interest in Fleet Street, which in turn has increasingly become in many important cases the subsidiary interest of multi-national giants.

This narration is not nostalgia for the days of Britain's grandeur and world-wide prestige. It is meant as a modest contribution to politico-journalistic history, for without a first-hand understanding of the pressures and influences which shaped the Lobby throughout those crucial years of change it is impossible to appreciate the different role of the political journalist of today and how it relates to a Parliament preoccupied with domestic affairs and problems, with only an occasional glance beyond the White Cliffs. When this book was being prepared for the printers I had a final check with the authorities of Parliament on the world status, if any, of the Lobby of today. They told me that the famous papers and overseas agencies of international reputation still have their names on the List but the correspondents themselves seldom enter the precincts, except for a few old-timers passing through London anxious to look up old friends. For news which will be of some interest to their readers back home they go elsewhere. One example illustrates the point: when James Callaghan was Foreign Secretary, just before he became Prime Minister, an international affairs debate was arranged, the first for over two years. Only a handful of MPs remained in the Chamber to hear him survey the modern world. Of Ambassadors in the Diplomatic Gallery there were none, and of newspapermen and women in the Foreign Press Gallery there were five.

The departure of the former powerful international corps brought compensations. Whereas the physical space in the members' lobby used to be so overcrowded most days by foreign and Commonwealth Pressmen pursuing sources and contacts, the House authorities found it impossible to admit the UK evening papers outside Fleet Street or the political-literary weeklies; while the Sunday papers were then so numerous that their political writers were admitted only one afternoon each week, from Tuesday to Friday on a rota system. (Where are they now, alas, the dear old familiar titles like the *Sunday Referee*, *Weekly Dispatch*, *Sunday Chronicle*, *Sunday Graphic*, *Sunday Empire News* and others?) When it was clear that the world correspondents had gone for good apart from occasional visits to the Press Gallery, but seldom the Lobby, the authorities decided to admit the evening papers' Lobbymen (in the early 1950s) and the Sundays and weeklies. The character of the Lobby has thus been reorientated from the global to the home base, although the overall total of active newshands in the Lobby has remained mainly unchanged.

Academic critics of the entire Lobby system complain that since the Press and Information Officers took over, the political correspondents have eagerly co-operated in the techniques perfected by Governments and Whitehall for news-management at all levels and the control of access to sources. In short, the indictment is that Lobby correspondents love the mumbo-jumbo of the secret society with its mystical formulas of unattributable, off-the-record sources which announce Cabinet decisions at second-hand but must never be identified. This is a distorted picture, and it is time that the record was set out. From the earliest days within my personal knowledge and experience, and confirmed by the Lobby records dating back to earlier years, the Lobby vigorously resisted the successive moves towards greater centralised control and group management, and opposed the various plans to formalise and organise all contacts on a central basis amenable to Whitehall's influence.

THE MIDDLEMEN

Following the appointment in 1931 of George Steward as the first official PRO and non-attributable spokesman at No. 10 Downing Street, similar appointments were made to all other Ministries and Departments. Old Lobby documents prove how suspiciously the Lobby viewed the experiment of interposing a new race of middlemen between correspondents and their traditional sources—Ministers, Permanent Secretaries and the Ministers' private offices and personal staff. The Lobby's annual report for that year (1931) said: 'Definite times were arranged for conferences and a room was provided at No 10 for meetings.' So the Lobby correspondents were *in* for the first time on a regular basis. This marked the beginning of the end of the old system, and the introduction of a new formula for the organised group meetings and corporate briefings by central Ministerial and Whitehall sources. On the surface it looked like a brave new world of open Government. In practice, it meant the very opposite. Despite the showpiece, the change of power and status was implicit; the old-style competitive 'outsiders' were converted into a fraternity of organised 'insiders'.

Though the formalised relations between Government and Lobby as part of 'the system' did not take place until 1931, the newsmen had been inside No 10 previously but not as regulars. The first time was during the General Strike in 1926. After Cabinet meetings during the grave crisis Ministers found themselves being lobbied vigorously by Lobbymen, as well as having to pass through milling crowds of angry strikers. To avoid the risk of contradicting each other in 'off-the-cuff' comments—on Lord Melbourne's dictum that 'it doesn't matter what we say so long as we say the same thing'—the Cabinet decided that during the emergency a Cabinet secretary should give 'guidance' to the political correspondents. The experiment was repeated on other major crisis situations, but never on a regularised basis until 1931.

In my time Ramsay MacDonald was the first Prime Minister to introduce regular but informal meetings with Lobby correspondents, handpicked because he had known some of us personally for some years. These were relaxed social and personal chats, far removed from the formal, politically geared sessions which became the set style in later years. Neville Chamberlain was the first PM to try to shape the Lobby as an arm of Government in pursuance of his appeasement policies. He disliked being confronted by unexpected off-the-cuff questions, so he proposed that we should submit them in detail forty-eight hours in advance. In consequence, his meetings with the Lobby lacked spontaneity and became set-pieces to enable him to elaborate his appeasement convictions.

Not that the Lobby correspondents in 1931 rejoiced at the prospects of easier living at Whitehall's news-tap. They were suspicious about where the novel policy of open door at No. 10 might land them. Let me quote, for example, from the 1932 Lobby report which, while giving a guarded welcome to the new initiatives in Whitehall, commented that 'it carries with it certain dangers. There is a danger that it may become too much a personal service of Prime Ministers and ignore the wider and more important sphere of Government information.' And as for making easier the access to the sources of power and decision, Ministers and Permanent Secretaries, the report added: 'This may be one of the consequences of an active development of the service which cannot be overlooked when considering the desirability of its continuance.' My old Lobby colleagues were fifty years ahead of their time! Within a year their fears were confirmed: when the Lobby formally protested against George Steward organising a Lobby meeting on his own initiative for a Minister, foreshadowing the future trend of centralised management and control of news. After the tensions of those early days, largely identical to the problems being experienced today, the Lobby's annual report of 1933 recorded that Mr Steward, when replying to the newsmen's anxieties about the way things were going, explained that 'although he was formally appointed to act for the Prime Minister and the Treasury, he was also required to act for the Government as a whole in all matters of a general character'. In his view, 'requests for meetings with Ministers should be transmitted through him at No 10 Downing Street but if he failed to obtain the Minister's promise of an interview he would then have no objection to the Lobby taking whatever steps were considered necessary'. To round off this record of the state of affairs at the time, I quote this further extract from the minutes: 'It was agreed to inform Mr Steward that the Lobby reserved their right to make direct approaches to any Minister and could not accept *any Press Officer* (my italics) as the only channel of communication between themselves as individuals and the Government.' This insistence on the supremacy of individual as opposed to group lobbying should be noted, because the modern centralised system of controlling Press contacts is the master key in the machine which keeps news, and access to news, under rigid control at the centre. Governments have not retreated a single inch since those early Lobby protests, despite their frequent promises about the need for more 'open Government' in the modern age, with lip-service tributes to the freedom of the Press as basic to a well-informed public opinion—transient escapes into fantasy from their real world of news-management and controlled access.

The period under review saw the real battles over the newspapermen's right to know. The annual Lobby reports over several years in the 1930s complained strongly about the frequency with which the political correspondents were threatened with the Official Secrets Act to discover the sources of leaks embarrassing to the Cabinet and Departments, and just as regularly the Lobby protested to the Prime Ministers and their Law Officers about the measures taken to intimidate newsmen. (These many incidents were in addition to the case of Jack Kirk, political correspondent of the *New-Chronicle*, who was grilled for five hours by the Special Branch of Scotland Yard to discover the source of his leak of a major Cabinet decision.*)

The above quotations from the old Lobby records are as relevant today as they were fifty years ago. The earlier generation of Lobbymen identified the dangers with great foresight, and their prophecies of the menace of the new despotism in controlling news and its sources have stood the test of time. It cannot be pretended that in the intervening years Fleet Street and the Lobby have made any real progress towards more open Government. Indeed, the system was much more open during my first two decades as a Lobby newsman than it is today. Then Ministers, the Permanent Secretaries and the civil servants in the Ministers' private offices were much more accessible and responsible to individual Lobby contacts than is conceivable today.

The present day openness of Washington, where a correspondent can get through on a direct line to a senior civil servant and where officials regard being helpful to newsmen as part of their daily routine, is not unlike that of Westminster in London in the pre-war and immediate post-war years. Since then the media have lost valuable ground in independent access to the sources where the real decisions are taken. Contacts with the faceless men of power are more complex and investigation is more difficult than yesteryear.

* Recalled in greater detail in the author's *The Abuse of Power* (W. H. Allen, 1978).

139

Of course, MPs in the mass have never liked the Lobby system, largely because they see it as a rival and privileged sector in Parliamentary life, being fed information secretly which is denied those on the floor of the House. Journalists have never been liked, and this is as it should be because the primary interests of Governments and politicians in relation to the media are irreconcilable. I remember during the time when the Lobby was moving to its modern group identity, a number of back-bench MPs under Sir Herbert Williams used to mount a constant watch by rota system on the political correspondents' meeting-room in order to identify Ministers attending the meetings. The details of the information members of the Cabinet passed on could easily be identified from the Press within hours; this in turn prompted questions in the Commons about the propriety of Ministers telling secrets to Fleet Street which had not been disclosed to MPs. Their purpose was to scare Ministers for breaching Parliamentary privilege, the subject which never fails to intimidate Ministers, officials and the Press. Incredibly bizarre efforts are frequently made to escape becoming involved in this crime of crimes against Parliament's commandments. One experience illustrates the point. In my very early days a former Secretary for Scotland confided in me the main findings of the report by the Committee of Privileges which had just approved the final draft a few minutes before. The details are long forgotten. The issues dealt with were topical and highly controversial, and my report of the findings was widely displayed all over the Kemsley papers, then comprising six morning and nine evening papers outside London. When, the following morning, I offered to share my big news with William Alison, a close friend but much more senior—he was the famous political correspondent of the London *Evening Standard* when the paper had a high political gearing under Lord Beaverbrook—I was warned of my imminent danger. A major breach of the Privileges law, he advised me, was made much worse by the fact that my crime involved the Committee of Privileges itself, the highest court of all. My only hope to avoid being incarcerated in the Tower, or at least making a mandatory maiden speech of abject apology on the floor of the House, after being rebuked by Mr Speaker, was to prevent Parliament, and troublesome MPs in particular, from seeing the evidence. So for the next twenty-four hours I kept vigil in New Palace Yard, the transport square under Big Ben, collecting all copies of Kemsley papers being delivered by messengers and newspaper vans for the libraries, reading rooms and tea-rooms at Westminster. I collected hundreds of these papers containing the exclusive forecasts of the Committee's findings, and piled them in my writing room in the Gallery. Frantic calls from local MPs (and the librarians) to the London office complaining that the home-town papers had not been delivered and demanding instant despatch by special messengers added to the confusion. It was all high farce, but after twenty-four hours I was safe. Official complaint about an alleged breach must be made to the Speaker within twenty-four hours and I had successfully played out time.

The following day some unfriendly MPs went to the Speaker to inform him in advance that they proposed to raise my report as a grave breach. But Mr Speaker Morrison (later Lord Dunrossil), an old friend of mine and not unaware of how I had 'seized' all papers destined for MPs' edification, rescued me from the dock by insisting that he was bound by the rules of the House which demanded that any complaint about an alleged breach must be raised on the same day. I recount this old story not to reassure anxious readers how a brilliant career almost ended before it had barely started but to illustrate the comic nature of the mumbo-jumbo which still prevails at Westminster and how a youngster cocked a snook at the majesty of the rules—and survived. The story about this author's fortuitous escape, thanks to the Speaker's sympathetic blind eye, from exposure in the Parliamentary stocks, illustrates how ridiculous the Privileges law has become.

All experience confirms that authority at all levels has no understanding of and no sympathy with the freedom of the Press and its need for access to information. I recount two hitherto unknown and unreported attempts made by all-powerful mandarins to censor even Parliament itself and to suppress Ministerial guidance to Lobby correspondents. In the early days of the Second World War Parliament, with an all-party Coalition under Sir Winston Churchill, provided its own unofficial Opposition formed by Earl Winterton, then 'Father' of the House of Commons, and Emanuel Shinwell (later Lord Shinwell)—they became known as 'Arsenic and Old Lace' after the successful play then running in the West End. Their criticisms of Churchill and his Government were often vehement and biting. The censors at the Ministry of Information 'blacked out' all such attacks because they considered the criticisms contravened the Defence Regulations prohibiting talk which caused 'gloom and despondency'. The idea of censoring Parliament when the country was fighting for freedom was patently grotesque. Protests were made by the Press Gallery and Lobby, and Lord Beaverbrook, then a member of Churchill's Cabinet, was given the task of reconciling the conflict and preserving freedom of speech and criticism already suppressed all over Europe by Hitler and Mussolini. Beaverbrook met a few of us over lunch at the Dorchester to search for a peace formula. Finally he recommended to Churchill and the Ministry of Information that there must not be any censorship of Parliament. Winston Churchill, who never could tolerate criticism, solved the problem to suit himself. He frequently used the system of secret sittings of Parliament, and whenever he sensed that the critics were to be in pursuit over his conduct of the war he never failed to offer a secret session. This enabled censorship to be total. Whenever Parliament 'spied strangers' and went into secret session it was a serious crime for a paper to report what had been said behind the locked doors. This was how Parliament applied censorship by 'the back door'.

Another extraordinary instance of censorship also involved the bureaucracy of the Ministry of Information. At the most crucial period in the war Britain's Intelligence discovered that Hitler was preparing to launch his 'flying bombs', pilotless planes loaded with explosives, and his V2s, the first of the guided missiles. Afraid of the impact on the people's morale of these mysterious bombing machines the Cabinet authorised the Minister of Information, Brendan Bracken (later Lord Bracken), to start preparing public opinion for the new bombing horrors then imminent. Bracken gave briefings to the Lobby on the well-established formula of non-attributable reporting: that is, the Lobbymen reported the grave portents but without identifying the authority and source of their reports. Once again the Westminster reports were totally censored by the MoI because they would depress the people's morale. Once more protests were made, again Beaverbrook was brought in as honest broker. The censors proposed they should in future sit in at all ministerial meetings and briefings with the Lobby. The Lobby refused to allow such official intervention. In the end the Ministry ruled that Lobby reports must be accorded their unique freedom not to identify sources.

NEED FOR MODERNISATION

Like Parliament itself, the Lobby has been strongly resistant to change and modernisation. It has not altered in any significant degree during the last hundred years, since it first assumed its present form and identity in the 1880s. Its continuity is unique in world journalism, its status has remained high, its professional standards an example to the modern media. It is a unique institution peculiar only to the British system. It is full of contradictions, riddled by hypocrisy, a ritualistic mystery, yet it has worked with notable efficiency and success despite what its detractors deride as the mumbo-jumbo of a secret journalist sect practising weird acts under the signs of the Zodiac. If the Lobby had never existed it would have been necessary to invent it to satisfy the British Parliamentary system. Indeed, it has spawned an endless series of 'Lobby terms' groups enthusiastically imitating the mysteries of the craft. Diplomatic, education, finance, health, trade union, industrial, City, social services, defence, home affairs, environment, transport, farm, food, and many other categories of specialist correspondents have their own groupings and rules, inspired by the identical theme: they all practise the Lobby code of conduct. They meet Ministers central to their professional jobs at highly confidential, off-the-record meetings and lunches, when the members of the Cabinet confide their secrets, policies, and problems. Such exchanges are protected by the sanctity of non-attributable sources, with solemn pledges that nothing will ever be given of those sources: on classic 'Lobby terms'. The shorthand 'term' simply means that the information conveyed on 'Lobby terms' may be freely used but only on condition that it is not attributed in any way to the informant but used on the responsibility of the reporter. 'I can state on the highest authority' is the professional and transparent euphemism to conceal the set needs of acceptable plagiarism.

This is not merely a case-history of working journalists clubbing together to organise their professional lives as a form of mutual protection cover to make life easier for themselves. Editors, too, have got into the act. Indeed, for my money, theirs is the tightest Lobby cult of all. Prime Ministers long ago discovered the technique of reinforcing the Official Secrets Act by the simple subterfuge of appearing to breach it themselves. When in trouble Prime Ministers of all parties, as part of Whitehall's bush telegraph system passed on from generation to generation, are invariably advised to send for favoured and favourable editors to come to No. 10 where they confide what euphemistically might be termed as secrets, subtly creating the illusion that they are seeking counsel and comfort in their hour of travail. The technique never fails. Two Prime Ministers boasted to me of the professional skills of dealing with editors. Editors, they said, are not case-hardened in dealing daily with Prime Ministers and their wily ways and sophistries, and are thus more readily flattered by the earnestness with which the PMs appear to lay some of their cards on the table and ask the best way to play the hand. I remember once asking one of my former editors, who had been invited to join an urgent safari to Downing Street, if I might have a brief minute from his file of what the Prime Minister had said, on non-attributable Lobby terms of course, for my future guidance. 'Oh no, James, I'm sorry but I can't. I'd love to really, but he insisted he was talking to us on Lobby terms. You see, if ever you were to hint, however indirectly, his background guidance I'd be blamed for leaking.' That's how to hook 'em and grass 'em, the biggest fish in the Fleet Street pool. In short, all levels of the media, from the humblest to the mightiest, are engaged in one vast conspiracy of compulsory plagiarism—while the sources which inspire news and editorials remain unmentionable.

Of course, the Lobby system for reporting political news from Westminster and Whitehall cannot conceivably go on as it is. It has been over-taken by history, it has been outmoded by the vast revolution in modern communications. The system needs modernisation, albeit at the price of some of the ritualistic observances which earned the devotion and dedi-cation of devout worshippers at the shrine for so many years. The crux of the problem lies in the traditional rules over organised group or corporate meetings of the Lobby. This is the area of the necessary plagiarism which all must practise. The informant and sources are concealed behind many allusions and illusions: 'I have it on the best authority'; 'In well-informed Government sources the claim was being made . . .'; 'According to the most reliable quarters'; 'Circles close to the Prime Minister insisted last night . . .' and so on, in endless permutations. It is all part of a confidence trick; the Prime Minister, Opposition leaders, Ministers and officials move their lips at the Lobby meetings but the words come out as the newsman's very own in a quick ventriloquist act. Everybody in the vast communications media knows who's been talking to whom, politicians identify the sources without difficulty, Fleet Street knows within minutes who has been talking to 'The Lobby'. This nonsense must stop. It no longer makes sense. As *the Press* has been transmogrified into *the media*, to include TV and Radio, the system has become farcical and archaic to meet modern needs and pressures.

Its present composition makes the Lobby ripe for reform. I recalled ear-lier that when I started at Westminster there were forty-five political correspondents *on* the British Lobby List and entitled to attend UK Lobby meetings. In addition, there were fifty Dominion, Empire, USA and other overseas newsmen *in* the Lobby regularly (but unable to attend the UK Lobby meetings). So the grand total was on the hundred mark. The overall total today is practically identical, but the character has changed. The number of chief political correspondents, the top men, remains practically the same at forty-seven; in addition, there are as many others variously identified, as deputies, number twos, alternates, assistants: these supplementary categories share all the rights and privi-leges of the senior men, the only restriction being that two Lobbymen from the same paper are not supposed to be in the Lobby at the same time in order to avoid overcrowding. The composition of the Lobby today mir-rors the contractions of the newspaper industry and the mighty explosion on eye and ear by the many TV and Radio networks. Of the total Press Gallery journalists in daily attendance, about a quarter from TV and Radio, and most of these are in the Lobby as well.

'FREE ENTERPRISE' LOBBYMEN
When all are present at Lobby meetings at Westminster, No 10 or else-

where in Whitehall, the so-called briefings and confidential guidance sessions look like a mass meeting. Gone is the former intimacy and confidentiality, and nobody expects the Prime Minister or anybody else to talk freely and frankly when so many people are in attendance. This poses many problems for newsmen. My own experience may be relevant. As the former political correspondent of *The Sunday Times* I never attended a single Lobby group meeting for many years before I retired. I did not attend the group meetings because Lobby meetings in modern conditions serve little value except for those with urgent deadlines, cameras and microphones to catch; those who need to know the daily run of the mill . . . who is speaking when, and what; what sort of motion will be put down; party attitudes, in short, routine news. For my part, I usually devoted the time to meeting two or three Ministers individually and alone, every week, with similar attention to Shadow Ministers as well. This was not, I duly discovered, an idiosyncratic belief of an odd fellow like me. I was in the good company of two of the most distinguished political writers among my contemporaries, acting independently but from common conviction. Take first David Wood, who was successively political correspondent, then political editor and later (and currently) European editor of *The Times*. On being appointed to the Lobby he was surprised to discover the amount of collectivisation of political news which had been developed within the system, ostensibly for mutual convenience but in reality much more for the convenience of the Executive than for journalists. For the *pro forma* style of news release it was tailor-made to cover the routine mechanics of distribution, but for discovering the substance or meaning of what was happening behind the controlled news items it was pointless. So Wood decided that for him (as for me and a few others) the groupist system was over-organised and stage-managed, and he gave up attending Lobby meetings for two main reasons. First, he had other more valuable sources than could be provided by the No. 10 spokesman acting on his remit. Secondly, he was convinced that from the Macmillan era onwards the Lobby had over-co-operated in its blatant news-management. After all, as he said to me years later, 'the No. 10 PRO is paid to protect the PM and his Government. That's no damned use to us as newshawks, we are not party hacks.'

This was no throwaway line. Wood made it a professional rule never to stand for any elective or honorific post in Lobby or Gallery. He also refused to pay his annual subscription to the Lobby organisation. For his pains some elderly fellow, overcome by being allowed to be close to authority, actually moved at a Lobby business meeting that Wood be excommunicated by the true believers. Both of us remained convinced for years that a third friend privately paid Wood's subscription in order to prevent

145

some ridiculous blood sacrifice being offered under tribal rites!

But James Margach and David Wood had an even more illustrious colleague cocking a snook at Whitehall's controlling access to news and comment. It is still universally agreed that Hugh Massingham of the *Observer* was the most scintillating of all political writers. Every Sunday morning he made politics enormous fun, unlike today's solemn editorialising. He never attended a single Lobby meeting in his long and happy life. He would never have found his way to the secret Lobby meeting place in the upper committee corridor, even if he had known of its existence. What the PM of the day or anybody else said 'off the record' at Lobby meetings was irrelevant. So far as he was concerned that was but the skin not the sausage-meet of politics. He was the greatest loner I have known. He established his personal contacts with Ministers and political personalities of importance on his own. The modern idea of four or five buddies getting together to entertain a Minister at a Soho restaurant was alien to his methods. He used to tell me that his father, the great Liberal editor, used to entertain Churchill, Lloyd George, Asquith and the famous at his own home, and went to their homes in return. That was how Hugh was brought up to deal with power and politics at the top, and that was how he continued. I cannot think of anyone operating in that fashion today.

I discovered from him the importance of cultivating the distaff side of politics. For several years Massingham recounted in his *Observer* pieces what took place at the Cabinet meetings every week, a highly personalised account of what everybody said, a count-down of what looked like the Cabinet minutes. No. 10's official spokesman of the day (Francis Williams, later Lord Francis-Williams) confided to me that Massingham's diaries of the Cabinet secrets were so accurate that even the security and intelligence experts were called in to discover the source of the constant inspired leaking. Close checks were made on the distribution of Cabinet documents; even expertly doctored papers, with slips and inaccuracies worked in, were channelled to suspected Ministers to see if the errors might be repeated in the Massingham version. All such counter-espionage traps failed to spring. Years later I discovered the source. Every Friday afternoon he had tea at a movable rendezvous with Lady Cripps. She was devoted to advancing the career of Sir Stafford Cripps and wanted him to become Prime Minister. Cripps, one of the three most powerful Ministers in the first Attlee Government, confided to his wife what had been happening. In due course she reported to Massingham what Attlee, Herbert Morrison, Aneurin Bevan and Ernest Bevin had said. The story confirms the judgment that good Lobbying is essentially a one-man business. Certainly I like to think I made good mileage myself out of the Massingham example of how individual free enterprise must never exclude the value of studying political housewifery.

The combination of all branches of the media at what are supposed to be confidential meetings covered by the mystic signs of 'off-the-record', 'for-guidance-only' and 'not for attribution' has made a nonsense of the system when today TV and radio dominate the pace of instant presentation. The Prime Minister, if one cites 'the highest authority available' in the little piece of ventriloquism, may attend a Lobby meeting where he talks freely on the traditional 'non-attributable' basis. The newspapermen write their reports on the usual background basis, using their own but not invoking the PM's authority. Within hours the Prime Minister appears on a TV or radio network interview or current affairs programme where he repeats for millions of viewers and listeners the very words he used non-attributably at the Lobby meeting a few hours previously. Political correspondents sit eagerly round the sets, taking urgent shorthand notes of the PM's words (which they have used as their own in earlier editions of their papers) and re-write their reports for the final prints quoting the Prime Minister in what he said on this or that network answering this or that interviewer.

The charade must stop. Clearly the Lobby must go 'on the record' and 'go public' if it is to keep its place in the communications world of today and tomorrow. This would encourage stronger reforms to modernise the old procedures of Parliament, also overtaken by history, and of the working of the British political system. In theory the decision already exists for the necessary updating. In May 1977 the Lobby, by forty-two votes to eleven, decided that meetings between Lobby journalists and Ministers may in future 'go on record' if mutually agreed. This was the decision in principle reached after a rumpus over allegations that an anonymous No. 10 spokesman had suggested that Sir Peter Ramsbotham, British Ambassador in Washington, was being replaced by Prime Minister Callaghan's son-in-law, Peter Jay, because he was a 'fuddy-duddy' and 'an old-fashioned snob', out of tune with the 'new young abrasive world of President Carter'. The rights and wrongs of the row are immaterial, although the experience illustrates how artificial 'non-attributable' comments become when there is no longer any mystery or secrecy about the source. It is of marked importance to note in this context that this strong move towards 'on-the-record' briefings was moved by David Holmes, political editor of the BBC and Lobby chairman at the time, someone in sympathy with the pressures to modernise the communications world at Westminster and for more openness and frankness. David Holmes's initiative opened the door wide for future meetings with Prime Ministers and others to become quotable. In theory it marked a notable advance of any importance 'on the record'. On one small-time occasion it was tried out, but it proved so trivial that no one noticed the difference!

THE FUTURE

If all this shadow-boxing were of interest only to a group of news-papermen and women earning their daily bread at Westminster with a professional self-interest in good relations with the Govern-ment-Whitehall Establishment there would be no need for anyone to lose a moment's sleep in worrying about modernisation. But the issues lie much deeper than that: they are at the very heart of the modern imperative for the people to be kept constantly informed, *in the open*, of what is happening in their name. There were earlier attempts to trans-form the Lobby from its non-attributable mechanics to an on-the-record basis. Sir Donald Maitland, when he was PRO to Edward Heath at No. 10, favoured the idea of the daily off-the-record Lobby briefings being replaced by open Press conferences in Whitehall (the lecture room at the Royal United Services Institution was earmarked as the ideal venue). Like many colleagues of the time, I was all for the reform provided that the system was to be genuinely open, with no reservations giving No. 10 and not the Lobby the privilege of deciding when to switch from on-the-record pronouncements to off-the-record guidance. Nothing came of the Maitland ideas because experiments tried by Prime Minister Heath— which enabled the PM to present two TV spectaculars dressed up as Press conferences—failed. They had imported the worst features (see below) of the Presidential Press conferences in Washington and Paris without any of the advantages of openness.

Here, the judgment of an experienced international journalist may be cited in support. Louis Heren, deputy editor of *The Times* and for many years his paper's Washington correspondent, has given a highly critical description of the much-vaunted Washington showpiece. About the role of journalists on such occasions, he has written: 'They were often bit players in the charade of the Presidential Press conference put on to pro-vide the illusion of a President in a dialogue with the Press.' The evidence from Washington helps to explain why the Heath experiment has never been repeated by his successors. The role of bit men with walk-on parts, in an exercise designed to concentrate the spotlights on the Prime Minister in a TV theatre showpiece, did not appeal to Lobbymen. Lobby meetings intended to go 'on the record' must be 'for real', under the control of the Lobby chairman and committee, and not used as an artificially created set-piece in news-management.

Joe Haines, when he was Press Secretary to Sir Harold Wilson, de-cided after a period of tension with the Lobby to discontinue daily group briefings. He posed the question 'whether a daily meeting between the Prime Minister's spokesman and political journalists on a non-attributable basis is good for the Government, good for the Press, and above all good for the general public which sustains us both. In my firm opinion, and in the view of the Prime Minister, it is not. I think many people rightly suspect the validity of stories which lean heavily upon thin air. From now on, it will be my general rule that if a statement needs to be made on behalf of the Prime Minister, that statement will be made on the record.'

The experiment in trying to create a brave new world in Government-Press relations had only a brief run, and when James Callaghan succeeded Harold Wilson shortly afterwards the information plant at once reverted to its old traditional 'Lobby terms' pattern, rejecting any hybrid grafting.

When the contemporary pressures for a modernised and more open Lobby system finally succeed, an important role will still remain for confidential background meetings between Prime Ministers, Cabinet Ministers, and top Whitehall experts and political writers. The whole character of political journalism has been transformed in the past ten or twenty years. Riding in tandem with the political/Lobby correspondents concerned with the urgency and immediate impact of events are the modern categories like analysts, commentators, columnists and editorial writers who are interested mainly in the developments and policy discussions preceding the final news announcements before the media. Their role cannot be satisfied by any mechanistic reforms moving the Lobby from the 'non-attributable' to the 'on the record'. The investigative job must be done in Whitehall, not Westminster. In Washington, for instance, despite the more open methods and direct access to top sources, the system of what is described there as selective 'backgrounders' is in constant service, the Lobby-style euphemisms widely practised, with studied refinements to conceal when a 'very high authority' or a 'high Presidential (or Departmental) adviser' was really the President or his chief aide, the Secretary of State, the Chief of the Treasury, and so on, talking on the mystical 'Lobby terms' to this or that favoured correspondent in the White House corps. There is considerable scope for this development in Whitehall, too, because of the pressures for more background information when major policies are in their formative period. The media and the country remain singularly ignorant of the decision-making processes in Whitehall and how the alternatives open are examined.

With the British Empire gone and Britain's status as a world power but a memory—and the certainty that the EEC Commission in Brussels and the directly elected European Parliament and any possible Scottish and

149

Welsh Assemblies will increasingly demand and acquire more power—the importance of Westminster will diminish even further. This will also reduce its significance as a source of major news. Inevitably this process will pose problems for the political correspondents if they are to retain their premier status in Fleet Street and elsewhere in the media. There is nothing novel in this dilemma. The eclipse of Empire and Commonwealth, and its consequences for Britain, brought a serious slump in the status and authority of the diplomatic correspondents who formerly operated on a global scale. To face head-on the dangers inherent and implicit in the decline of Westminster, the Lobby—and the varied groups who also make a living out of writing and talking about politics—must go where the real power has gone, and that is to Whitehall.

This is where the future lies for them. Peter Hennessy, of *The Times*, has demonstrated most impressively over recent years how it is possible to penetrate the veils of secrecy in Whitehall and to produce a constant flow of news reports and commentaries about what is really happening in the exercise of power. He has done so by by-passing the usual political and Press information channels, by digging constantly and patiently in the Executive's inner defences. One can foresee that in the near future Hennessy will be chief of a team of colleagues who will be allotted different groups of Departments for their investigative energies.

This is precisely the area where the political correspondents can establish their status and authority in new dimensions now that Westminster had become more circumscribed in decline. My judgment is reinforced by a much more substantial source. James Reston, of the *New York Times*, has written: 'The power of the Executive to decide things in secret is growing all the time; what reporters have to do is to move in much earlier in the development of policy . . . (by) aggressive reporting during the drafting process so there can be debate before it is too late.' He signposts the way ahead for the Westminster corps as well.

The change should not prove painful. Already within the Lobby two categories of Lobby journalists function. This is the result of the enormous increase in the volume of reports, documents and information papers which originate from within the huge Government and State administrative bureaucracies which have a direct impact upon the public and form a substantial part of Government and State information. But this side of the business is ancilliary to the primary role of Lobby/political correspondents who must remain pre-eminently concerned with power and its execution at all levels. There are thus two groups emerging following parallel courses. The mountain of reports and documents of a routine character may well be left as the specialist concern of the deputies, assistants or alternates within the Lobby. This should free the senior men to concentrate on power and policies—and conflicts—where they matter and where the decisions are taken in secret: inside the complex of Government, Executive, Whitehall—but not at Westminster or in Parliament.

Such reforms in the Lobby system, and the new directions and enterprises now inevitable, would in practice mirror the changes which have already taken place in the Government's Information Service. Of the 1,500 Information and Press Officers only around thirty deal with 'the Lobby' as such, on the old terms, providing the major liaison between individual Government ministers and the political newsmen; the remainder concentrate on providing the wider sweep of Government information and seldom meet a Lobby correspondent. It suits the mutual interests of Government and Fleet Street for Whitehall to use the available Lobby machinery for distributing advance copies of several hundred documents and reports every year—'advance releases' as they are described—as it is a convenience for all media offices to read the columnous mass of words over the preceding day or two and then prepare the reports for readers, viewers and listeners.

Such reforms in the working of the Lobby system—meeting in particular the opportunity of on-the-record reporting of hitherto unnamed anonymous sources and the realignment of responsibilities within the corps to take account of the modern role of Lobby work at different levels—would at the same time enable the senior correspondents to concentrate most of their energies on what has become the most neglected area of all: the need for more behind-the-scenes lobbying by personal contact *inside* Whitehall to investigate the decision-making processes and inter-departmental pressures which precede the final Cabinet decisions and announcements. This is the next challenge. The opportunities obviously exist. The leaks demand exploitation. It is worth noting that the *Railway Gazette* was responsible for discovering and publishing a secret Departmental document on transport and *New Society* for acquiring and publishing a Cabinet paper on child benefits; while *Private Eye* first exposed the evidence which finally led to the Poulson corruption case as the spin-off from politics and local government. These were all politically explosive stories, but they came from non-Lobby sources. The way ahead for a modernised Lobby system beckons with rich promise: reporting of politics from Westminster and Whitehall will become even more crucial in an educated democracy—and the Lobby must remain the main source.

If the Lobby were able to do its job properly, with uninhibited access to the decision-makers, there would be no need for tinkering around with a Public Information Act or making trifling changes in the Official Secrets Act which would only have the effect of tightening secrecy over crucial sectors while creating the illusion of a liberalising advance towards more disclosure. A modern democracy can only survive through a free Press and media in an open society—and in this ideal the Lobby must be in the forefront—not sharing the glory and cares of Government but in healthy conflict with the Establishment. And, in Walter Lippmann's phrase, to bring its searchlight to bear on public issues. Lobbymen do not pretend they have the divine right to be told on a plate of what took place at Cabinet, but they have the right and the duty to try to discover what precisely went on.

The Lobby has been left with only one small sector so total has been the revolution brought by the vast throughput of Government and State communications. As I mentioned earlier, only about thirty Information and Press Officers deal with 'the Lobby' in the old specialised sense; the remainder deal directly with the media and the public. To give but one example of the magnitude of the communications exercise maintained by Whitehall, the Central Office of Information—it was the first integrated inter-departmental service, established in 1949, anywhere in the world—delivers annually on behalf of Government Departments and itself eight thousand individual reports, documents, statements, announcements, etc., direct to Fleet Street, TV and radio network offices; and each of the eight thousand information statements or State news reports may have one thousand to two thousand copies taken for mass distribution. That is the scale of information and instant communications at the disposal of the modern State.

The CoI has a staff of 1,200 specialists spread through its branches for communicating information to people: advertising (State budget of £15 million), exhibitions, publicity, publications and design, films and TV, photo services. Its reputation abroad is high: the direct services to South America, Canada, United States, Singapore, Japan, the Middle East and Europe are valued for their importance and integrity. The highly professional staffs perform their duties with loyalty to their Departments and Ministries. Departments and Ministries are the arms of Governments, and Governments are political party creations. This diversion to spell out the gigantic scale of the world of communications and information at the disposal of Government underlines the imperatives for the Lobby increasingly to assert its adversary role with Government and State—the more so since Parliament itself has been deprived of so much of its authority over the Executive in the modern 'elective dictatorship'.

The power-game dice of the 'off the record' unattributable guidance 'on Lobby terms' are heftily loaded in favour of the Prime Minister, Ministers, Opposition leaders and other figures. If the Lobbyman takes the credit for reporting the 'guidance' vouchsafed to him from on high as his own revelation and discovery, he has no reason under the code for protesting about betrayal when the Minister rats after the heat is on him. Alas, I can confirm that this is a constant occupational hazard of our business. Ministers are never conscience-stricken when they deny as a lot of lies what they have just passed on privately as the true gospel. Two examples of this form of political cynicism can be given from the experience of George Clark, political correspondent of *The Times* and Chairman of the Lobby when this book was being prepared for publication, whose prestige the author invokes as the best contemporary authority.

The first instance concerns a personal meeting with Richard Crossman when Clark had sensed something big was happening behind the scenes. As Secretary of State for Social Services Crossman had delayed the introduction of charges on teeth and spectacles provided under the National Health Service (the charges were promised in the 1969 Budget). Clark had previously discovered that a group of backbench Labour MPs had gone to protest to Crossman and had told him they would vote against the charges. Crossman told Clark that he had delayed the Order for this very reason. He also said that he was not going to follow the road taken by Barbara Castle, as Employment Secretary, who had been forced to drop in humiliating fashion her 'In Place of Strife' legislation because she had not taken account of back-bench opinion.

When the row exploded in the Commons Crossman called Clark every type of liar under the sun and protested violently that he (Crossman) could not conceivably have been the source. In his famous *Diaries* Crossman duly claimed that he had only told Clark that the timing of the Order's introduction was a matter for the Chief Whip and Leader of the Commons to fit into the business programme. A different story from the real record indeed. Several years later Crossman confessed to Clark: 'Sorry about the teeth and spectacles, George. Although there was nothing much wrong with your story, I had to "murder" you in the House for political reasons.' A journalist's reputation is always the first and easiest to sacrifice, for the poor fellow is inhibited by his code of honour from throwing chapter and verse at the Minister.

The second example of how a Lobby correspondent may be thrown to the wolves occurred at the 1978 Labour Party conference. Prime Minister James Callaghan listed four subjects which would have priority in the impending Parliamentary session and mentioned that, subject to the Royal Commission on the National Health Service, the Government proposed to rectify the blunders made by the earlier Conservative Government in their reorganisation. Clark lobbied a Minister and a senior civil servant who were members of the Departmental team. On their authority Clark reported that the Government planned to remove one tier of the Health Service organisation because it was overweighted by administrators. The Area Boards were to be abolished. When the row broke in the House, with MPs repeatedly quoting the information leaked to Clark, David Ennals, the Secretary of State, denied vehemently that any of his Ministers or officials had ever spoken to *The Times* man and that the report was totally untrue!

George Clark, by far the most experienced of the present generation of political correspondents, believes with David Wood, Hugh Massingham and James Margach that the corporate-style regular meetings have little value in modern conditions except for the routine flow of hand-out information. By all means have Lobby meetings on the record, as open Press conferences. Little of substance would then emerge anyway! Then, he says, Lobbymen and women would get back to their basics, with lobbying done individually of individual Ministers and MPs—the further from Whitehall's eyes and ears the better.

The political correspondent has the most difficult and challenging role in the entire world of communications because of this adversary situation, the inherent conflict over what the public interest demands: the Prime Minister and Cabinet convinced they are its guardians through the maximum secrecy and security, while the reporter seeks for the hidden realities of power, extracting the maximum of that information which the authorities are most anxious to withhold. Winston Churchill, always hypersensitive to criticisms and leaks, provided the text which all Prime Ministers eagerly follow. One day, when berating his Cabinet colleagues about talking too much to Lobby correspondents, he warned, according to Cabinet papers: 'Experience has shown that leakages of information have often occurred as the result of skilful piecing together by representatives of the Press of isolated scraps of information, each, in itself, apparently of little importance, gathered from several sources. The only safe rule, is, therefore, never to mention such matters, even in the form of guarded allusions, except to those who must be informed of them for reasons of State, until the time has come when disclosure in whole or in part is authorised. I am prepared to recognise that reasons of State may require, in appropriate cases, the confidential communication of some information to a responsible editor or Lobby correspondent, for purpose of guidance; but such communications are only justified where it can be ensured that the question of confidence and the terms on which it is given are respected.'

The message, from Winston and all Prime Ministers, never varies: they are always anxious to pay lip-service to the ideal of an open and informed society but are never prepared to pay the price that essential facts which they are convinced should remain secret in the State's interests (and very often their own) should come to the knowledge of public opinion through disclosure. They prefer the politics of secrecy. And 'secrecy is the real English disease', wrote Richard Crossman, years before his *Diaries* tried the cure.

The paradox in today's democratic state is that the more complex and sophisticated modern communications have developed the more secretive Prime Ministers and Governments of all parties have become. Constant appearances on TV networks do not advance more open Government, but rather the reverse, because these by their nature are concerned with images and not communication and information. So the Lobby correspondent has the crucial role in the vast new world of communication and power. He is at the heart of the unending inter-action and conflict between Government and the governed, and has the most subtle role of all. He is at the centre of a triangle of power and conflict of interest: between the Government's need to preserve secrecy, the public's right to know what's being done in its name, and the newsman's first duty to discover the facts and reveal them, thus defeating the State's obsessional secrecy.

In this exercise the Lobby has a special mission. Westminster is no longer the source of power. Power has gone to Downing Street, the Cabinet, the Whitehall-Executive dynasty, all basically anti-disclosure, pro-secrecy, anti-media. The Lobby has to go where the new focus of power has gone: it must penetrate and defeat the institutionalised and negative control and management of news and information, and not least the secret working of the system. For the Lobby must never be seen as a corporate state, flattered as part of the Establishment. It is basically a lot of people caught up in the vast world of communications. Its purpose is to serve readers, viewers and listeners with the first urgent draft of history the very moment it happens. Finally, I am in no doubt that the Lobby itself will assert a new initiative and develop a new challenge and mission as it launches itself into its second century. The next hundred years beckon with the promise of new horizons.

INDEX

Abdication crisis, 111, 113–4

Adams, David, 72

Adams, David Morgan, 72

Agriculture, harmonising State and private enterprise in, 91

Alison, William, 140

Allen, Sir Douglas, *later* Baron, 87

American Committee system, 83

Amery, Leopold, 57, 116

Anderson, Sir John, *see* Waverley, John Anderson, 1st Viscount

Appeasement, mass revulsion by people against, 112

Armstrong of Sanderstead, William Armstrong, Baron, 87; advice to Permananent Secretaries, 87

Asquith, Herbert Henry, 1st Earl of Oxford and Asquith, 9f., 23, 24, 35, 39; 'Wee Frees', 31 and *n.*

Asquith of Yarnbury, Lady, 113, 114, 117–8

Atholl, Duchess of, 119–20, 122; referred to as 'Red Duchess', 121

Attlee, Clement Richard, 1st Earl, 3–4, 9, 11ff., 21, 32, 36–7, 39, 45, 57, 71–2, 117f.: blessed with extreme luck, 4; possessor of instant instinct for power and leadership, 10; herculean courage of, 11; outstanding in elusive art of managing men, 14; master in businesslike tough management in running Cabinets, 14; one of 20th century outstanding peace-time Premiers, 18; de-stylised manner of, 20; created rapport with working classes, 20; triumph of, 22; streak of cruelty in make-up, 25; unfeeling toughness of, 25; his heartlessness, 25–6; misjudgement in timing of retirement, 36–7; illness, 41, 51; suffers stroke, 52

Attlee Brigade, 100; formation of, 100

Avon, Anthony Eden, 1st Earl of, 7f., 11, 15f., 33, 36ff., 39, 45, 79f., 116f., 135: tragic failure of, 8–9, 16; loyalty to Conservative Party, 33; intransigence of, 34; illness, 41; plagued by ill-health, 51–2; resignation as Foreign Secretary, 114; criticism of Neville Chamberlain and Stanley Baldwin, 115; popularity of in Conservative Party, 115; no unity with Sir Winston Churchill, 115

Baldwin, Stanley, 6ff., 13, 19f., 23–4, 28ff., 34, 39, 42, 50, 55ff., 63–4, 68, 79, 102, 105ff., 11, 132: phenomenal luck involved in achieving power, 6; possessor of instant instinct for power and leadership, 10; herculean courage of, 11; extreme personality of leadership exhibited by, 11; the nation's ideal Prime Minister, 17; one of 20th century outstanding peace-time Premiers, 18; frankness of, 21; success, 23; calculated ruthlessness of, 25; detestation of Lloyd George, 25; difficult to understand, 29; disillusioned by intake of new generation of Tories, 31–2; views on maximum length of Prime Ministership, 39

Balfour, Arthur James, 1st Earl of, 18

Bancroft, Sir Ian, 87

157